W9-DJF-237

NEW DIRECTIONS FOR ADULT AND CONTINUING EDUCATION

Susan Imel, *Ohio State University*
EDITOR-IN-CHIEF

Adult Learning in Community

David S. Stein
Ohio State University

Susan Imel
Ohio State University

EDITORS

Number 95, Fall 2002

JOSSEY-BASS
San Francisco

ADULT LEARNING IN COMMUNITY
David S. Stein, Susan Imel (eds.)
New Directions for Adult and Continuing Education, no. 95
Susan Imel, Editor-in-Chief

Microfilm copies of issues and articles are available in 16mm and 35mm, as well as microfiche in 105mm, through University Microfilms Inc., 300 North Zeeb Road, Ann Arbor, Michigan 48106-1346.

ISSN 1052-2891   electronic ISSN 1536-0717   ISBN 0-7879-6323-2

NEW DIRECTIONS FOR ADULT AND CONTINUING EDUCATION is part of The Jossey-Bass Higher and Adult Education Series and is published quarterly by Wiley Subscription Services, Inc., a Wiley company, at Jossey-Bass, 989 Market Street, San Francisco, California 94103-1741. Periodicals postage paid at San Francisco, California, and at additional mailing offices. Postmaster: Send address changes to New Directions for Adult and Continuing Education, Jossey-Bass, 989 Market Street, San Francisco, California, 94103-1741.

SUBSCRIPTIONS cost $65.00 for individuals and $135.00 for institutions, agencies, and libraries.

EDITORIAL CORRESPONDENCE should be sent to the Editor-in-Chief, Susan Imel, ERIC/ACVE, 1900 Kenny Road, Columbus, Ohio 43210-1090. e-mail: imel.l@osu.edu.

Cover photograph by Wernher Krutein/PHOTOVAULT © 1990.

www.josseybass.com

Printed in the United States of America on acid-free recycled paper containing at least 20 percent postconsumer waste.

Contents

EDITORS' NOTES   1
David S. Stein, Susan Imel

1. Learning Community History   5
Jane M. Hugo
What are learning communities, and what is their potential to effect
social change? This author traces the definition of and development of
learning in community through an examination of the adult education
literature. Definitions and uses of learning in community are critically
analyzed to illustrate the forces influencing learning and community.

2. Creating Local Knowledge Through Learning in Community: 27
A Case Study
David S. Stein
This chapter describes how community residents come together to study
and create local knowledge. Knowledge emerges from the actions and
interactions of the learning group with its community. The author pro-
poses a six-stage process describing how a group learns in community.

3. For the Common Good: Learning Through Interagency   41
Collaboration
Susan Imel, Cynthia J. Zengler
Communities of practice can emerge from collaborative activities. In
this chapter, the authors describe how interagency partnerships facilitate learning, and they examine the connection between collaborative
groups and learning.

4. Organizational Learning Communities and the Dark Side of   51
the Learning Organization
Phillip H. Owenby
What are the limitations of learning organizations? In what ways do
organizations control the learning process? This chapter takes another
look at learning organizations and suggests how organizations can
encourage members to learn together in ways that promote true organizational growth.

5. Negotiating Power and Politics in Practitioner Inquiry   61
Communities
Cassandra Drennon
The facilitator has been a factor in adult learning groups. Drennon inves-
tigates the ways in which a facilitator can block or hinder learner growth.
The tension between creating democratic learning spaces and maintain-
ing control is discussed as a reflective practice for adult educators.

6. Learning Communities in Remote Retreat Settings 73
Gretchen T. Bersch, Carole L. Lund
Discussions about learning communities usually focus on the learner and the learning process. Bersch and Lund discuss the influence of context in forming and sustaining learning communities. The context in this case is a retreat setting.

7. A Small Circle of Friends: Cohort Groups as Learning 83
Communities
Randee Lipson Lawrence
Learning in a cohort group is the theme of this chapter. The author investigates how cohort group learning influences instruction, the learning space, and the creation of knowledge webs.

8. Adult Learning in Community: Themes and Threads 93
David S. Stein, Susan Imel
Several themes and patterns emerging from the various chapters in this volume are presented. Four of them in particular illustrate the power of learning in community to effect individual, organizational, and civic change.

INDEX 98

EDITORS' NOTES

Although the concept of learning communities has emerged in the higher education literature, the topic has seldom been discussed in adult education. We describe learning in community as individuals coming together to exercise control and influence over the direction, content, and purposes of their learning. Learning in community is marked by characteristics noted by Ulrich (1998), the most important of which are a strong group identity, expectations for participation and contribution, and working toward the greater good. Ulrich describes these associations as communities of values rather than as communities of proximity. The learning community becomes the site of stored collective thought and is sustained by the development of "wisdom capital" (Gaudiani, 1998, p. 59). *Community* refers to the sustainable connection between individuals brought about by a shared interest, sense of purpose, or need. *Learning* is the product of shared dialogue, action, and reflection on action.

We consider learning in community to occur outside formal educational institutions through the efforts of ordinary individuals with or without the intervention of adult educators. The focus is not on individual learning but on the common understandings that are created by the community and increase the collective understanding of a situation. In civic, educational, governmental, and business entities, learning in community becomes a means for taking action on issues important to the commonweal. Unique features of this form of learning is the voluntary nature of participation, the sharing of teaching and learning roles by the members, and the change in the community and in the individual members that is brought about by collective meanings and actions. Whereas the notion of adults engaging in learning with each other is certainly not new (Stubblefield and Keane, 1994), the salons and taverns have now been replaced by study circles, chat rooms, coffeehouses, and community centers. The desire to share ideas, understand daily events, and engage in civic or communal action remains, however. Learning in community expresses the desire of adults to engage with and learn with and from one another.

In this sourcebook, learning in community will have wide-ranging descriptions. It may be organized by place when a community forms a council or by space when employees gather to discuss practice issues or individuals become a network to share in a single purpose. This sourcebook will explore how learning communities form, the processes that guide learning in a particular community, and the actions resulting from the learning. The chapters are organized by the places where the learning community forms as well as by the type of learning, such as learning among friends.

New Directions for Adult and Continuing Education, no. 95, Fall 2002 © Wiley Periodicals, Inc.

Learning in informal communities has been a defining feature of adult education. In Chapter One, Jane Hugo highlights some historical themes of learning in community. She also provides an overview of different types of relationships between community and the education of adults and the field of adult education in the United States. By providing a historical review of learning communities, she sheds light on their current forms.

Chapters Two and Three look at learning in civic environments where community needs drive the learning. In Chapter Two, David Stein describes how community issues—specifically the need to improve quality of life—foster the development of learning in community. In Chapter Three, Susan Imel and Cynthia Zengler describe how communities of learning derive from the need for interagency collaboration. In both chapters learning is in the service of the community and is driven by community leaders who are living and working in the same physical space. By becoming skilled in understanding community issues, a sustainable learning community is developed. Although the members may change, the learning community persists.

In Chapter Four, Phillip Owenby questions the benefits of organizational learning. Because organizations do not critically examine the ways in which they maintain hierarchical structures, power, and corporate interests, organizational learning may not be able to deal with the issues most important to their survival. Owenby presents a case of how organizational learning did change the culture of power and raise political consciousness. In Chapter Five, Cassandra Drennon focuses on practitioner networks as learning communities. Of special interest here is the role of the facilitator, and particularly her ability to negotiate the group's power relationships and politics. Like Owenby, Drennon looks at the organizational constraints that may deter learning in community.

Friends using a space for learning is examined in Chapters Six and Seven. In Chapter Six, Gretchen Bersch and Carole Lund focus on the remote retreat setting and its connection to fostering learning in community. They examine the relationship between the learning that is accomplished, the environment in which it occurs, and the friendships that form as a result of the experience. In Chapter Seven, Randee Lipson Lawrence examines how members of a cohort learning group in higher education come together as friends to create a sustainable learning community. She shows how friends can cooperatively learn and foster the spirit of learning while transcending physical space. She uses the metaphor of weaving knowledge webs to describe the connections among the group that allow for multiple knowledge sources.

The last chapter discusses the common themes that run through this volume. We see a future in which communities, in both their geographical and social configurations, form to deal with the challenges of lifelong learning and confront the struggles of promoting and sustaining opportunities to use learning for the common good. Despite the emergence of electronic forms of communication, face-to-face learning in community will persist as adults struggle to find meaning in their own lives and the civic, social, and work environments in which they reside.

References

Gaudiani, C. "Wisdom as Capital in Prosperous Communities." In F. Hesselbein, M. Goldsmith, R. Beckhard, and R. Schubert (eds.), *The Community of the Future.* San Francisco: Jossey-Bass, 1998.

Stubblefield, H., and Keane, P. *Adult Education in the American Experience: From the Colonial Period to the Present.* San Francisco: Jossey-Bass, 1994.

Ulrich, D. "Six Practices for Creating Communities of Value, Not Proximity." In F. Hesselbein, M. Goldsmith, R. Beckhard, and R. Schubert (eds.), *The Community of the Future.* San Francisco: Jossey-Bass, 1998.

David S. Stein
Susan Imel
Editors

DAVID S. STEIN, *associate professor of adult education and workforce development at The Ohio State University, College of Education, has worked extensively with local health departments and community agencies to promote participative learning and action research strategies.*

SUSAN IMEL, *a senior research specialist at the Center on Education and Training for Employment, The Ohio State University, College of Education, directs projects including the ERIC Clearinghouse on Adult, Career, and Vocational Education.*

1

There are deeply rooted connections between learning and community in adult education. The historical examples and issues discussed here shed light on the interactions between individual learning, community, and modern society.

Learning Community History

Jane M. Hugo

The relationship between learning and community is a central theme in the history of adult education. Since the early twentieth century, social theorists and adult education practitioners have mourned or railed against the demise of community relationships and targeted geographical communities for educational interventions in order to increase civic intelligence and social control. Adult educators have studied the dynamics of community power and done community needs analyses. Educators and community leaders have designed educational programs to link community resources. Adult education historians have celebrated the breadth and number of learning groups but also suggested that professional adult educators might rationalize away their significant efforts. Others who have felt a loss of community have tried to recapture it in encounter groups, grassroots social movements, and cyberspace (see, for example, Brookfield, 1983; Jarvis, 1985; Taylor, Rockhill, and Fieldhouse, 1985; Stubblefield, 1988; Stubblefield and Keane, 1994; Palloff and Pratt, 1999).

According to Stephen Brookfield (1983), the word *community* "has the power to inspire a reverential suspension of critical judgment in the minds of adult educators, social workers, and those in the caring and health professions." He goes on to note that the word seems to imbue one's work "with a humanistic concern and an almost self-righteous compassion which preempts any considered analysis of its central features." He cites Maria Effrate, an American writer on community work, as saying that community is, "like motherhood and apple pie, . . . synonymous with virtue and desirability" (p. 60).

Ralf St. Clair (1998) agrees that community is central to adult education. But he argues that what is needed is a new approach that captures "the diversity, disjuncture, and relations of power which communities represent"

NEW DIRECTIONS FOR ADULT AND CONTINUING EDUCATION, no. 95, Fall 2002 © Wiley Periodicals, Inc.

(p. 5). He looks at the agency of individuals in communities. The learning that takes place there, St. Clair contends, would be better understood if educators viewed community as a site of tension between structure and action, a middle ground between the individual and society, a form of relationship (that is, interlocking networks) rather than a shared identity or geographic place. Political scientist Robert Putnam's (2000) research on the bridging and bonding social capital that is accrued through social networks or lost in their absence provides one such view. My own work on nineteenth- and twentieth-century women's nonformal study groups suggests that learning in community is a complex, multilayered, and often contradictory process (Hugo, 1996, 2001). Personal relationships, ties to community-as-place, and wider social issues all came into play simultaneously but in different ways over time.

This chapter reviews some of the historical themes associated with learning in community. It provides an overview of the varying relationships between community and the education of adults as well as with the field of adult education in the United States. Readers will see that community can be any or all of the following: a democratic social ideal, an emotional foundation for the learning process, a laboratory for adult life concerns, a power structure with which to reckon, and a site for learning's fulfillment.

The chapter begins with a discussion of three historiographic issues related to studying learning in community. It then briefly describes historical currents that began in the Progressive Era and continue to shape our understanding of learning in communities. Next it outlines three historical variations of learning in community. The chapter concludes by illustrating how an ecological approach to understanding learning communities helps us look to the past to understand its influence on their present forms.

Finding a Usable Past for Learning in Community: Historiographic Issues

The story of adult learning in community is influenced by three historiographic issues: definitional concerns, a dominant yet ahistorical analysis of social change that has shaped the definition of community for social scientists and historians, and the problematic nature of historical evidence of learning communities.

Definitional Concerns. *Adult learning, adult education, learning in adulthood,* and *community* are all imprecise terms made more so by additional descriptors such as *formal, nonformal, informal, situated, liberal, liberating,* and *context-based.* Several histories of adult education have been criticized for their imprecise definitions, resulting in accounts that either confound categories or claim almost every human activity as adult education (Rose, 1995; Wilson, 1995). As a result, *learning community* may refer to groups, locales, weak or strong emotional ties in a group, and qualities of participatory democracy in action.

Who gets to define learning in communities or communities of learners is of further concern. Social power and privilege influence how people read and write about learning communities. For example, an early adult education historian, C. Hartley Gratton (1955), believed that women's educational groups added to the "range and bulk" of adult education without increasing its "depth and penetration." Their existence was encouraging, he noted, but he hoped that one day they could be "improved into more solid adult education" (pp. 257–258). Feminist historians and educators struggled against patriarchy and established canons in the last half of the twentieth century to render women's educational work visible (see, for example, Scott, 1991).

Dominant Yet Distorted Conceptions of Community. The search for a usable past for learning and communities often builds on the traditional community-versus-modern-society dichotomy. This *gemeinschaft* (community)-*gesellschaft* (society) continuum is a common social-change typology used in history and other social sciences. It is based on ideas put forth by nineteenth-century German scholar Ferdinand Tönnies. According to Thomas Bender (1978), Tönnies's ideas became firmly embedded in historical and sociological thinking, influencing how people understand both community and society in modern life.

Tönnies explored changing social relations in the context of rising capitalism and the urbanization of society. In 1887, he saw the social relations of urban, industrialized areas coming to dominate. As an ideal, *community,* or *gemeinschaft,* has qualities of intimacy, emotional bonds, mutuality, embracing the wholeness of individuals' lives, and group solidarity that one might find in a family, kinship or friendship networks, and small towns or neighborhoods. Community is an end unto itself (Bender, 1978), not a means to something else. Solidarity is a hallmark of communal relationships, although conflict is still possible. But, according to Bender, it is "mediated by emotional bonds" (p. 8).

In contrast, an associational or organizational form of society, or *gesellschaft,* is characterized by the image of the city—urban, competitive, heterogeneous, impersonal, secular, superficial, transitory, and fragmented. Society is market-oriented in a way that allows economies to operate independently from the relational networks that once linked trade. Bureaucratization and centralization are additional hallmarks. Science and technology have new authority (Bender, 1978). An observer back in 1903 felt that the "metropolis" made the modern mind "more calculating, rational, and intellectual" (Jarvis, 1985, p. 151). *Gesellschaft* offered a release from all the constraining features of face-to-face relationships critical to *gemeinschaft* (for example, intolerance and denial of access to sources of power).

In Bender's (1978) opinion, Tönnies saw *gemeinschaft* and *gesellschaft*— community and society—as "'two kinds of human collective living' in which all individuals are involved." They coexist throughout time and have a reciprocal relationship. "From this perspective," writes Bender, "community is not a specific space or mere baseline for historical change; it is a fundamental and enduring form of social interaction" (p. 43).

Many influential historians and contributors to the emerging field of sociology found Tönnies's conceptual framework useful but ended up defining it more in terms of polarities, marking the direction of change rather than reciprocal, ongoing phenomena. As a result of this distortion, the historical and sociological analyses of the transition from rural to urban life got trapped by an ahistorical "logic of collapse" (Bender, 1978, p. 11). According to this logic, as a society became more urbanized, community relations weakened and the experience of community disappeared. *gemeinschaft-gesellschaft* thus came to represent an understanding that social change was a developmental, sequential, unidirectional phenomenon. A culture was either modern or traditional, either urban or rural. Movement from *gemeinschaft* to *gesellschaft* was evidence of evolutionary progress, suggesting a "logic of uniform growth" (p. 53).

Bender asserts that this distortion of the coexistence and interaction of *gemeinschaft* and *gesellschaft* has had two consequences worth noting for our consideration of learning communities. First, historians and social scientists too often fail to look for the tension and interaction between the two types of social interaction, believing that community is a thing of the past rather than an experience that undergoes transformation in relation to society. Second, a nostalgia for community has led social scientists to try to graft community arrangements onto large-scale organizations or ascribe them to place-based social activity "regardless of the quality of human relationships that characterize these contexts" (1978, p. 143). These mismatches disguise the real distinctions between community and society. An emphasis on the reclamation of collapsed community distracts people from fully understanding the public culture (made possible by mass media, industrialization, bureaucratization, and technological advances) that is its social counterpart.

Despite historical evidence to the contrary, a popular sentiment persists that community is a thing of the past—a victim of modernity (Bender, 1978; Putnam, 2000). Jarvis (1985) notes that during the 1960s and early 1970s, sociologists viewed the loss of community as a very bad thing. Anything that engendered the rediscovery of community was "widely regarded with approbation" (p. 152). During the twentieth century, adult education as a field and society at large were affected by the presumed loss of community and attempts to rediscover or re-create *gemeinschaft*-type societies (Jarvis, 1985; Imel, 2001). A desire for an experience of community in the context of learning was evident in the 1980s and 1990s. Studies looking at adult learners' metaphors for adult education identified "family" as a particularly salient image, underscoring their longing for a caring and supportive environment characterized by a sense of community, trust, and mutual respect (Deshler, 1985; Proctor, 1991). Business and industry have been exploring the strategic use of learning communities to maintain competitiveness in a global, knowledge-based economy (Imel, 2001).

Historical scholarship that analyzed the interaction between community and society would, in Bender's (1978) estimation, throw light on how to achieve balance in modern social relations. "The task of the cultural historian or critic is not to date the moment when one of the worlds of social relations is replaced by the other; it is to probe their interaction and to assess their relative salience to people's lives in specific situations" (p. 43). Readers of learning-in-community historical narratives need to be attentive to the legacies of collapse and nostalgia. They likewise need to be attentive to the interaction between community and society attended to in histories and in present-day efforts to recognize, constitute, reframe, or renew learning communities.

Evidence of Learning Communities. It is difficult to find a usable past for learning communities for two reasons. First, the historical evidence of learning in community is disparate and possibly quite ephemeral. Communities of learners may not be oriented to written documentation, may not have education as a primary goal, or may operate in a virtual medium, like today's Internet. Brookfield (1983) observes that in contemporary Western industrial societies, where pluralism and mobility are more and more the norm, "cohesive groupings may be empirically unobservable" (p. 62). As a result, some educators have set aside an understanding of community in the earlier place-based sense in favor of what is more clearly observable—namely, communities of interest (for example, Apple computer users or hip-hop fans) and communities of function or practice (for example, teachers, business owners, or social workers) (Brookfield, 1983; Imel, 2001).

Second, to understand the relationship between learning and community we need to gather evidence not only of the existence of learning communities and the techniques used to support their work but also of their social contexts. Educational historian Lawrence Cremin urges historians to think about an "ecology of education" (1989, p. viii), a changing, complex formation of "configurations of education" (1976, p. 30) made up of many political, pedagogical, or personal relationships in a given social and intellectual context. Nonschool sites of learning, which Daniel Borstein called "habitats of knowledge" (Cremin, 1988, p. 438), are of particular interest because of their role in popularizing learning and education and the alternative avenues to learning they afford people. If we want to understand the educational effect and significance of learning communities, we must not only look at individual institutions and individual variables but also at "the ways in which they pattern themselves and relate to one another" and "the ways in which their outcomes confirm, complement, or contradict one another" (p. 128). The evidence that historians gather may be different if, in Bender's view, they ask about the equilibrium between community and society, focusing on the "tension and interaction rather than on collapse" (1978, p. 119).

My exploration of the educational ecology of a hundred-year-old women's study club, the Coterie, led me to members' diaries and papers, newspaper clippings, club programs, club minutes, national women's organization records, photographs, church records, participant observations, interviews with members, and numerous secondary sources (Hugo, 1996). This research shed light on the members' and the club's web of local and translocal social ties between 1885 and 1985. It allowed me to draw conclusions about important dimensions of this one learning community, including the balance between social control and individuality; group restraints and supports; the kind of knowledge that has been privileged; gender, race, and class influences; and the degree to which this learning community is rooted in local and national contexts and is subject to larger social concerns in addition to the concerns of its individual members.

Historical Currents That Shaped Understandings of Adult Learning in Community

The relationship between adult learning and community has roots in religious, scientific, philosophical, and social movement traditions. Despite the positive connotations of the concept of community, in fact a learning community has the potential to be either radical or conservative, depending on it and the broader social context. Community forms of relationships can also be oppressive. For example, Robert Putnam (2000), in his landmark study *Bowling Alone: The Collapse and Revival of American Community,* discusses threats to individual liberty and tolerance that "might be hidden on the dark side of civic virtue" (p. 351).

Much of the U.S. discourse on adult learning in community today is a legacy of the Progressive Era, an intense period of social reform spanning the 1880s through the 1920s. In the face of a world war, increased immigration, scientific advancements, and social unrest at home and abroad, Americans experienced a number of cultural dislocations. As disillusionment, frustration, fear, cynicism, and iconoclasm grew, it was a time of reappraisal and change. "Some likened the times to having one foot on the relatively solid ground of established habits and the other on an escalator careening in several directions at a variety of speeds" (Hugo, 1996, p. 182). Education was one response to these dislocations.

The field of adult education in the United States has its intellectual footing in nineteenth to twentieth century theorizing about social change and the role of education in social conditions (Jarvis, 1985). According to Bender (1978), "Social theory in the nineteenth and twentieth centuries has been concerned with the problem of restating the value of community in an urban society increasingly dominated by large-scale organization" (p. 143). Thinkers from the fields of anthropology, psychology, and sociology highlighted issues of social control, order, and individuality in the movement from traditional to modern life (Stein, 1960; Jarvis, 1985). Progressive Era reformers in the early part of the twentieth century recognized the need to come to grips with modern, urban society. Indeed, historians of the period contend that one of the central dilemmas of reform work at that time was the need to cooperate with the emerging managerial, expert-driven, social-scientific models while also trying to "preserve human agency and other qualities of human individuality from the relentless forces of industrialization" (Sklar, 1995, p. 37; see also Susman, 1984).

Many of the women and men who were active in the formation of the U.S. adult education field believed that learning was a social process at the local and national levels. This group of late nineteenth- and early twentieth-century social theorists included Eduard Lindeman, Charles Horton Cooley, Jane Addams, James Harvey Robinson, W.E.B. Du Bois, Alain Leroy Locke, Mary Parker Follett, Joseph Hart, and John Dewey (see, for example, Bender, 1978; Stubblefield, 1988; Kett, 1994; Gyant, 1996; Potts, 1996; Rose, 1996). In keeping with mainstream Protestant-American values, these people had a strong faith in the power of education to improve the individual and society (Susman, 1984; Podeschi, 1986). They thought a community of fellowship made possible through adult education was vital to democracy and a needed counterbalance to society's values. Many fashioned their ideas out of discourses of reform in which social progress and human perfectibility were possible through *reform of* as well as *adjustment to* the emerging system (Susman, 1984; Taylor, Rockhill, and Fieldhouse, 1985; Stubblefield and Keane, 1994).

Eduard Lindeman's 1926 book *The Meaning of Adult Education* (Lindeman, 1961) reveals that several of these intellectual currents were at work in his ideas on the relationship between adult learning, community, and social change. He was concerned about such qualities of modern society as increased community fragmentation, a reliance on experts that resulted in the capitulation of thinking people, conformity wrought by standardization caused by rapid transportation and communication, and the impact of machines on people's sense of power, self-expression, freedom, creativity, appreciation, and friendship.

However, Lindeman (1961) did not wish to undo modernity. He saw in adult education, especially education in groups, the potential to "supply directive energy for collective enterprises" (p. 89) that were a "representation of individual interests" (p. 101). In short, adult education was "an agitating instrumentality" (p. 104) for improving oneself and the social order. "Adult education," he wrote, "specifically aims to train individuals for a more fruitful participation in their smaller collective units which do so much to mold significant experience. . . . Adult education is devoted to the task of training individuals in the 'art of transmuting . . . experience into influence' " (p. 38). The attention to both individual and social change was, in Lindeman's words, "the bilateral though unified purpose of adult learning" (p. 105).

Lindeman's vision of adult education flowed from his faith in the intelligence of the masses; he felt that their intellectual aspirations remained untapped by schools but could be awakened in community groups using methodologies free from the rigid pedagogical routines he saw in formal educational institutions. Although he did not use the terminology of learning communities, his vision of learning in the context of community contains many of the same qualities that contemporary educators strive for in learning communities. "Small groups of aspiring adults who desire to keep their minds fresh and vigorous," wrote Lindeman, "who begin to learn by confronting pertinent situations; who dig down into the reservoirs of their experience before resorting to texts and secondary facts; who are led in the discussion by teachers who are also searchers after wisdom and not oracles; this constitutes the setting for adult education, the modern quest for life's meaning" (1961, p. 7).

The historical wellsprings highlighted here are some of the forces that shaped the relationships between adult learning and community today. The next part of the chapter illuminates some of the paths carved out by these intellectual currents.

Three Historical Variations of Learning in Community

What sorts of learning communities have been portrayed in historical narratives of adult education and learning? Brookfield (1983) offers one useful way of classifying community learning groups: autonomous learning groups, community development groups, and community action groups. These describe important features and differences between learning communities, although, in reality, there is also overlap.

Autonomous Learning Groups. Most histories of adult learning or adult education in America reach back to the seventeenth and eighteenth centuries to identify groups of adults who spontaneously and voluntarily came together for the purpose of mutual improvement through common study. These included religious, literary, scientific, agricultural, and philosophical societies. One often-cited example is the elite Junto, a Philadelphia-based reading and discussion circle started by Benjamin Franklin in 1727. Others groups were part of elaborate efforts to quicken diffusion of useful knowledge to the general population (Gratton, 1955; Stubblefield and Keane, 1994; Kett, 1994). For instance, in 1826 Connecticut educator Josiah Holbrook started the Lyceum movement, a loose, national federation of local, county, and state study groups. Lyceums sprang up between 1830 and 1860. They tended to exclude discussion of politics and religion, stressed science and useful knowledge, and encouraged temperance and morality as well as the development of museums and libraries (Stubblefield and Keane, 1994). In theory, community people were to educate one another, avoiding overreliance on outside lecturers or "formal exercises" (p. 89). Between 1880 and 1920, the women's club movement added thousands of women's educational groups across the country.

An experience of community and a connection to society have been important in autonomous learning groups. Maria Rogers (1947), writing about a workshop panel and committee on autonomous groups at the 1947 annual meeting of the American Association for Adult Education, outlined ten characteristics of these groups. She highlighted a high degree of friendship and loyalty to the group, the group's influence in a community because of its longevity, the satisfactory fit between educational activities and members' needs, and the loss of a fear of social interaction because of the psychological safety of the group. "Due to the length of time these groups endure," wrote Rogers, " members develop genuine intercommunication, gain deep understanding of each other's personalities, points of view, use of language. . . . Growth of personality is a consequence of such experiences" (p. 176). She went on to assert that autonomous groups are vital because they help ensure that individuals adjust to social circumstances. They are thus important to democratic societies. They help form public opinion in any community and can change attitudes when that is necessary. Finally, autonomous groups are often the starting point for social movements.

Such locally organized, voluntary educational groups continue to form and disband today. A few examples of what some now call communities of practice (Marsick, Bitterman, and van der Veen, 2000) are model airplane clubs, investment groups, book clubs, and teacher inquiry groups. The sustainability of such groups is often connected to the commitment of a group of core members and the ongoing socialization of new members into the group. Over time, autonomous groups, like the Coterie mentioned earlier, achieve longevity if they remain relevant to successive member cohorts. For instance, between 1885 and 1985 the Coterie reinvented itself several times to maintain its intellectual basis for friendship—the holding together of diverse interests and a community of interests (Hugo, 1996). The local community of Fayetteville, New York, was always an important factor in the group's work—a learning resource, a site for collective action, and a link to tradition for transient residents—but the members' sense of community in the group changed over time as it re-created itself to be relevant to their lives. Early on, the group was a place for systematic continuing education when that was not available to women. Later it became a place for discussion of issues of the day before women had access to the public sphere. Still later it was a place for self-expression when members' lives were dominated by professional work or demanding volunteer work and they were going through a shift in identity because of changing roles.

Early adult educators faced a leadership conundrum when it came to autonomous learning groups. They were not sure how to serve, tap, or build on the diverse array of autonomous learning groups in any given geographic region when these groups had their own leadership traditions. Rogers (1947) recognized two types of autonomous groups—those formed to carry out social welfare or "social action" programs and those that subordinated civic action to companionship, cooperation, communication, and mutual improvement. She noted a degree of indifference and hostility on the part of professional educators toward this second type of group but warned them that they had a responsibility to create an atmosphere where such groups could "form and function freely" because they were a source of creative energy. Furthermore, there seemed to be a greater likelihood that ideas attractive to individuals in the relationship-oriented groups were put into practice, "thus making education vital" (p. 179).

Rogers's article points to other historical tensions between the practice of the public educating itself and adult education practitioners' leadership in educating the public. These tensions include the ability of groups to do their work without the intervention of professional adult educators; the role and relationship educators should play in autonomous groups; the power adult educators should or should not exercise in autonomous community groups; the value placed on group relationships to social action; and the balance between work with these groups of community learners and "the conventional type of adult education which recruits students by an appeal to 'interests' or objective 'purposes'" (p. 179). These tensions played and continue to play a part in the field's relationship to this variation of learning community.

Also of interest to those mapping adult learning in autonomous community groups is the influence of three other factors: the mass media; the participants' formal schooling experiences; and the participants' race, class, gender, and sexual orientation profile. Through books and magazines that groups use as information sources and their members' formal schooling experiences, they selectively appropriate the language and emphases of national cultural or educational trends to establish their own legitimacy. For example, the Coterie linked its work with the efficiency movement of the 1920s, the first and second waves of the women's movement in the 1920s and 1970s, and the expert-driven diffusion of knowledge in the 1930s (Hugo, 1996). Even without the intervention of professional adult educators, autonomous learning groups' learning choices are broadened or constrained by cultural forces.

Community Development Groups. Community-based initiatives designed by adult educators to improve or regenerate communities are the second type of learning community. In other words, these represent adult education in and of the community (Brookfield, 1983). Characteristics of community education include a focus on real-life problems identified by community residents, coordination of service delivery, community collaboration through shared resources, and links between home, school, and community.

Confronted with the social challenges of the Progressive Era, Americans realized that universal schooling had not prepared them to deal with the demands of industrialization, urbanization, and centralization.

Psychologists were divided about how to "produce persons capable of governing themselves" (Stubblefield, 1988, p. 131). Could intelligence be increased in adulthood? Was eugenics the answer? Was an "intellectual aristocracy" needed?

For Progressive Era thinkers and educators like Eduard Lindeman, Joseph Hart, Harry and Bonaro Overstreet, John Dewey, Jane Addams, Alexander Meiklejohn, and Ruth Kotinsky, the ideal of community was key, the foundation of democracy and adult education, the way to prepare adults to govern themselves. For instance, Hart judged that to attain that ideal the development of the "social imagination of individuals" was necessary. Drawing on emerging social sciences like sociology and psychology, educators like Hart believed that the one answer to social conflict and fragmentation was "new mind: mind that creates a solution that all the conflicting interests find more satisfactory to each one than any of their former partial answers was to anyone" (Hart, 1951, p. 125). This approach to learning in community stresses intellectual empowerment by "including larger and larger portions of the community in an intelligent direction of affairs" (Kotinsky, 1933). Rather than expecting to reestablish the *gemeinschaft* experience of small-town America, early twentieth-century proponents of community education talked about developing a social ideal of civic intelligence or social intellect to guide a society revolutionized by science, technology, and urbanization that was experiencing economic and political instability (Kett, 1994).

Historian Joseph Kett (1994) argues that although progressives trusted the direction of change, "they did not trust evolutionary laws to enact themselves" (p. 294). Educators were urged to lead the way in defining problems and proposing solutions. For example, Meiklejohn—the acknowledged father of the learning community movement in higher education—structured his Experimental College at the University of Wisconsin in the late 1920s on beliefs about how best to nurture the "social mind" and "national intelligence." Freshman- and sophomore-level college students and the faculty participated in a structured two-year program that eschewed disciplinary specialty based on electives, focusing instead on the common study of democracy in the Athens of the fifth century B.C. and in nineteenth- and twentieth- century America. Meiklejohn's approach revolved around classic books, discussions that lessened the distance between teacher and learner, community-based research patterned after the Lynds's influential *Middletown,* and an emphasis on students developing their views while also connecting those views to the real world (Stubblefield, 1988; Gabelnick, MacGregor, Matthews, and Smith, 1990).

These structured, cross-disciplinary interactions were to be an antidote to the fragmented, increasingly specialized groupings that characterized the university experience and formation for adult life. Meiklejohn thus tried to give college students experience with a reconstructed form of community life that would lead to more creative problem solving. Trained experts assumed a prominent role in this type of community development. In fact, Meiklejohn saw teachers not only as "servants of scholarship" but also "creators of the national intelligence" (Gabelnick, MacGregor, Matthews, and Smith, 1990, p. 12).

Some writers believe a community education movement arose early in the twentieth century whereas others place it in the 1970s (Knowles, 1980; Stubblefield, 1988; Kett, 1994). This movement organized the learning resources in communities and led to innovations like the development of community schools used by adults and children. It also promoted the resolution of community problems through educational processes and programming, such as study circles or public forums (Oliver, 1987). The social reconstruction potential of community education attracted the support of funders like the Carnegie Corporation in the 1920s and the Ford, Rockefeller, and Mott foundations in the 1930s and 1940s (Hiemstra, 1984; Stubblefield and Keane, 1994). Adult education efforts based on this community improvement model included immigrant learning groups at settlement houses such as Hull House in Chicago in the early 1900s, "moonlight schools" for literacy education in Kentucky and the Carolinas, experiments in African American education led by African American intellectuals, public health and cooperative extension demonstration projects, community theaters, and community and regional councils whose job it was to mobilize public opinion on issues of the day (Hiemstra, 1984; Kett, 1994; Guy, 1996; Gyant, 1996).

Educators in the 1920s were eager to sort out which community education techniques and technologies worked best to diffuse knowledge and modify social behavior (Kett, 1994). One common technique used to develop social intelligence was community deliberation, "brought about by organizing a group of people with expertise who represented the vital functions—not institutions—of the community" (Stubblefield, 1988, p. 127). Brookfield (1983), for example, describes the work of the Canadian *Farm Forum* radio programs (in the 1930s) that were a catalyst for local discussion groups. In addition, many rural British Columbia communities in the late 1950s and early 1960s participated in the *Living Room Learning* scheme sponsored by the University of British Columbia. Using print and audiovisual materials, the local, volunteer-led groups engaged in activities meant to help them improve their communication skills and understand their culture, think critically, and become more tolerant of differing ideas. The *Great Books* program, a reading and discussion scheme started in 1945 by Mortimer Adler and Robert Hutchins in the United States, was another print-based effort to develop and sustain community, a free society, and democracy (Brookfield, 1983). Some adult educators in the 1940s suggested that membership in discussion groups was a substitute for the neighborly relationships lost in urban development or manipulated through mass media (Essert, 1948).

The community development theme, with its emphasis on pragmatism and scientific methods, continued into the latter half of the twentieth century. The influential modern adult educator Malcolm Knowles (1980) carried forward some Progressive Era currents of community development. He believed community was a "format for learning"—that is, "a means to the end of helping individuals and communities learn how better to solve their problems" (p. 149). Knowles also continued the association of community development education with scientific approaches by calling communities "laboratories for learning" and organisms that could learn to deal with problems. Professors of adult education talked about "the educative community" (Hiemstra, 1984, 1985) and the community as "the natural setting for most adult and continuing education programs" (Hiemstra, 1984, p. 67). Texts discussing community education in the 1970s and 1980s highlighted adult educators' need for specialized knowledge and skills in community theory, needs assessment, group dynamics, the discussion method, curriculum development, program planning and evaluation, and resource development (Brookfield, 1983; Hiemstra, 1984, 1985). Facilitating community education projects required an understanding of the horizontal (that is, internal) and vertical (external) "pulls" affecting individuals in a community (Hiemstra, 1984). By strengthening the horizontal relationships in a community, adult educators would "facilitate a heightened sense of community" at the personal and collective levels (p. 68).

The relationships between community and adult learning in this second category can be messy, and some would argue, need to be questioned more critically. Brookfield (1983) observes that community development education "rests on a normative preference, often of the development worker or agency rather than of community members, as to what are the desired behaviors or improved attitudes" (p. 107). This caution has been amplified by those who critique the nature of community and learning in workplaces, which are perhaps the transmogrified arena for community development in the late twentieth and early twenty-first centuries. The workers are the equivalent of community residents. Human resource and training personnel have replaced the facilitative community developers. Proponents of learning organizations argue that they support continuous learning opportunities, promote inquiry and dialogue, encourage collaboration and team learning, empower participants toward a shared vision, connect the organization to its environment, and provide strategic leadership for learning (Marsick, Bitterman, and van der Veen, 2000). In contrast, historians such as Schied (2001) argue that this human relations discourse needs to be understood in the context of the scientific management and Taylorism of the early 1900s, the growth of corporate control of worker education through the two world wars, the threat to management of strong labor unions at the end of World War II, and the rise of human resource development professionals along with the popularity of human capital theory in the 1960s.

Zuboff (1988) argues that "learning is the new form of labor" (p. 395). In Schied's (2001) analysis, management seeks control over workers' knowledge. Learning is a product that must be "captured" from the knowledge makers through various systems and cycled back into the business. Using the rhetoric of learning communities in a workplace context may illustrate the inappropriate grafting of community onto organizations that Thomas Bender (1978) warned against. He believed it does not create true community and draws attention away from what is really happening under the guise of community building.

Community Action Groups. The history of adult education and adult learning in North America also includes examples of learning communities that moved beyond encouraging a more informed citizenry or modifying social behavior. These others have been committed to identifying underlying problems affecting geographic locales or social groups and solving them by taking action informed by new understandings. In short, these learning communities are less about restoring a lost harmony and more about social transformation. They are often aligned with burgeoning or established social movements such as the labor movement of the 1930s and 1940s, the environmental movement in the 1960s and 1970s, the civil rights movement of the 1950s and 1960s, the farm worker movement of the 1960s, and the women's peace movement throughout the twentieth century (Kornbluh, 1987; Alonso, 1993; Stubblefield and Keane, 1994). Adult education in this context "aims not only to inspire individual learners who acquire the knowledge needed to navigate the tumultuous waters of day-to-day life but also to enable those learners to conspire—to unite, melding their individual agendas in collaborative planning and collective action" (Heaney, 1996, p. 6).

The social democratic legacies of Lindeman, Dewey, Kotinsky, and other progressive thinkers from the 1920s and 1930s reverberate through discussions of this type of learning in community. Ruth Kotinsky (1933) said, "Adult education is not a random external accretion to the social body but an intimate part of the developing life of the nation" (p. 77). Decrying the tendency of the adult education field to give "mechanical answers to social situations" (p. 82), she urged her readers to move away from "schoolish things," characterized by "'indoor' grappling with 'outdoor' problems" (p. 82). Instead, the field should foster "an active grappling with realities, of which the 'indoor' activities will be real part and parcel, providing conditions for reflection and the formulation of plans and purposes to be used 'outdoors,' and felt to be needed by the 'outdoor' participants" (p. 108). Thus, problem-based education coupled with reflection and action would allow adults consciously to exercise control over the society in which they lived.

The community organizing work of Saul Alinsky in Chicago, the labor and civil rights work of Myles Horton, founder of the Highlander Folk School (now called the Highlander Research and Education Center) in

Tennessee, and the literacy work of Brazilian educator Paulo Freire are three often-cited examples. Adult education historians have begun to question previous "structured silences" in the field's history, and as a result other examples of community action work are becoming visible. Four such examples are Hilda Worthington Smith's labor education work in the 1930s at the Byrn Mawr Summer Schools for Women Workers and She-She-She Camps (Kornbluh, 1987), Dorothy Day and Peter Maurin's Catholic worker movement activities among the poor (Stubblefield and Keane, 1994), Marcus Garvey's work to bring to life an educational philosophy of self-ethnic reliance (Colin, 1996), and Septima Clark's leadership of voter registration efforts in the 1950s and 1960s through the citizenship schools (Stubblefield and Keane, 1994; Easter, 1996). All intentionally integrated learning into their community action work.

Heaney (1996) points out that adult education in the context of community action is "critical, but never the decisive factor in achieving social and political goals." "Essential to success," he asserts, " is the presence of a dynamic political apparatus—a collective, a union, a people's organization through which collective energy can be channeled and focused" (p. 57). Kotinksy (1933) believed that adult educators do not need to "create artificial groups to come and get education outside their normal milieu" but should instead "find its groups largely ready-made" (p. 186). Heaney (1992) notes that movements—"a dynamic fabric of interdependent nodes of action moving toward an emerging and shared vision of what can be"—create "within-reach possibilities for action" (p. 57). For this reason, we must try to understand community action groups in their historical moment, paying attention to social control mechanisms, crises that give rise to the need for action, group restraints and supports, disorganization and reorganization patterns, and transitions brought about by urbanization, industrialization, and bureaucratization (Stein, 1960).

Spurred on by Lindeman's exhortation to help individuals transmute experience into influence, the adult education field has historically put high value on educational enterprises that produce civic acts, propel a social movement, or build influential institutions. Leading-edge community action organizations like Highlander offer many insights into the workings of community action groups, but less influential learning communities can teach us as well. My research on the Coterie (Hugo, 1996) surfaced patterns of civic action that corresponded to Lindeman's (1961) "agitating instrumentality" (p. 104). At times the women's club studied and took collective action on a number of public health, education, women's rights, war, peace, and environmental issues. However, the group also chose not to pursue collective community action at other times. Changes in the political environment and movement networks affected the interplay of the women's personal, pedagogical, and sociopolitical realities. One stark example of this was the group's study of and support for America's involvement in World War II and its total silence on the Vietnam War. There was ample public support and infrastructure during the 1940s to help the Coterie act collectively, but the 1960s and 1970s did not offer the same ecology of education. As a learning community that fundamentally put the person first and the subject matter second, the Coterie had to negotiate social change and its own social cohesion (Hugo, 2001).

The location of action-oriented communities of learners in the mainstream or on the margins of adult education is a function of the interaction between larger social trends and development of the field of adult education (Heaney, 1996). Although community-based learning for social change was a central part of the early discourse on adult education in the 1920s, it lost currency in the face of several trends linked to the professionalization of the field and politics. These trends included the rise of scientific management and training in the first half of the twentieth century, the rejection of social analyses influenced by Marxist or socialist ideologies, the growth of knowledge in the psychology of group behavior and human relations from the 1930s through the 1950s, and the acceptance and implementation of Theodore W. Schultz's (1961) human capital theory in public policy and human resource and leadership development (Kett, 1994; Rose, 1996; Schied, 2001). However, since the 1980s there has been a resurgence of interest among professional adult educators in learning with a social change purpose. Work in popular education, feminist theory, and critical theory has led to increasing calls for revitalized adult education curriculum focused on transformation and learning to take action (Heaney, 1996; Lakes, 1997).

Community action groups take advantage of an "atmosphere" or historical space created by "special historical, political, social, cultural elements" (Horton and Freire, 1990, p. 92). For example, comparing Highlander's literacy work to that of contemporary literacy workers, Horton said, "They're at a disadvantage in that we were working in a really revolutionary situation. And they're in a low ebb-tide situation, where the going practice is to fall back on telling people that if they learn to read and write they'll get a job" (p. 92). They also noted that academics did not view Horton's practice of community work as education until Freire was exiled from Brazil (in 1964) and came to Harvard, where he started talking about and writing about the experience of out-of-school education. "And lo and behold," said Horton, "people started looking around and they said, 'Oh, you know maybe there is something outside schools we could call education.' And it was only then that people started saying Highlander was doing education" (Horton and Freire, 1990, p. 201).

There is a continuity of values in the historical examples presented earlier and the views of contemporary educators involved in learning communities to achieve greater social justice through structural change. These educators, says Hart (1990), make a "fundamental commitment to struggle against the blinding and distorting effects of power in as many ways as are appropriate or possible, and a commitment to help create nonoppressive communities" (p. 36). Like the other two variations, this one too bears critical reflection and analysis. Political correctness; tensions between the vision, the process, and community members' expectations; power dynamics; and the participants' risks related to consciousness raising and political action, for instance, need to be unpacked and examined in relation to participatory learning and community building (Brookfield, 1983; Campbell and Burnaby, 2001).

Conclusion

The history of learning communities suggests that we can better understand past and present attempts to link learning and community building when we contextualize the development and workings of learning communities—that is, when we take an ecological approach and view them in relation to several factors in their environment. There is a need for descriptive and comparative case studies that examine not the history of learning communities but rather how communities of adults "historically learned and under what conditions" (Wilson, 1995, p. 242). I offer two examples of how this approach might inform further study.

First, learning communities are one response to the shifting community (*gemeinschaft*)-society (*gesellschaft*) patterns of social interaction. Organizations, professional educators, and formal and informal leaders meld learning and the experience of community in order to strengthen connections between people, facilitate ability to keep up with the rapid social change that comes with industrial and scientific change, and right social injustices.

If we resist the myth of the collapse of community or nostalgia for some golden age of community, we can study the role and function of communal learning groups in negotiating or mediating the *gemeinschaft-gesellschaft* aspects of modern life (Bender, 1978). Several questions emerge. How do the two patterns affect learning groups and the problems they wish to solve through self-improvement, mutual improvement, or social action? Do men and women of different ethnicities, ages, and classes draw the boundaries around their learning communities in ways that are similar or different; what is included or excluded from the community? What qualities persist from older communal learning efforts? What new patterns are emerging? How do participants' multiple loyalties (for example, as union member, church member, citizen, and family member) affect the functioning of learning communities and networks of such groups? Under what historical conditions or circumstances do the demands of community and society exert more or less influence on learning groups? Where and how do learning communities form and flourish in bureaucratic institutions or societies?

Second, the leadership styles, functions, and techniques used in learning communities are historical artifacts, socially constructed solutions to situations adults face. They are the products of the interaction of a complex web of factors that include mainstream American values, competing educational philosophies, financial supporters' agendas, socioeconomic events, power relations organized by race, class, and gender, the growth of new academic disciplines, and public policy agendas.

This chapter's discussion of the three historical variations of learning communities identified some of the directions and tensions associated with leadership in community learning. For example, the professionalization of community learning work codified leadership expertise, such as program planning and group dynamics. But other community learning leadership styles developed separately from but in relation to professional adult education circles and formed distinct leadership traditions such as the maternal leadership associated with the so-called public homeplaces created by numerous women's organizations (Hugo, 1996; Belenky, Bond, and Weinstock, 1997). One tradition is not necessarily evil and the other good; both may do good work and both may entail compromises. However, situations like this alert us to issues of power, silencing, knowledge politics, social control, individual agency, and resistance.

Before we say an example of community learning is liberal or liberating, democratic or an exercise in social control, we need to examine critically the web of forces influencing leadership in the group or network. We need to ask how leadership is defined and by whom. What are the leadership's philosophical roots? From where does it draw its authority? How do learning community leaders negotiate individual growth and group solidarity? When emotional bonds, mutuality, and group solidarity are critical to a learning context, how do leaders and followers relate to each other? What happens when leadership mandates community learning? What leadership skills do learning communities need to be successful? What can we learn from other community learning leadership traditions that is invisible or marginalized in the field of adult education?

Struggling with questions like these will broaden and deepen our understanding of the relationship between learning and community. Some argue that the interest in linking learning and community building at this point in our history has much to do with an urgent need to address profound cultural changes at work globally. In a way, the present time has much in common with the Progressive Era, the founding period of adult education (Putnam, 2001). As Lindeman (1961) and others have imagined, learning communities and community learning initiatives have the potential to supply directive energy for individual and collective enterprises. Future historians will write the stories of how adults discovered and channeled that community energy.

References

Alonso, H. H. *Peace as a Women's Issue: A History of the U.S. Movement for World Peace and Women's Rights.* Syracuse, N.Y.: Syracuse University Press, 1993.

Belenky, M., Bond, L., and Weinstock, J. *A Tradition That Has No Name: Nurturing the Development of People, Families, and Communities.* New York: Basic Books, 1997.

Bender, T. *Community and Social Change in America.* New Brunswick, N.J.: Rutgers University Press, 1978.

Brookfield, S. *Adult Learners, Adult Education, and the Community.* New York: Teachers College Press, 1983.

Campbell, P., and Burnaby, B. (eds.). *Participatory Practices in Adult Education.* Hillsdale, N.J.: Erlbaum, 2001.

Colin, S.A.J. III. "Marcus Garvey: Africentric Adult Education for Self-Ethnic Reliance." In E. Peterson (ed.), *Freedom Road: Adult Education of African Americans.* Malabar, Fla.: Krieger, 1996.

Cremin, L. *Public Education.* The John Dewey Society Lecture #15. New York: Basic Books, 1976.

Cremin, L. *American Education: The Metropolitan Experience: 1876–1980.* New York: HarperCollins, 1988.

Cremin, L. *Popular Education and Its Discontents.* New York: HarperCollins, 1989.

Deshler, D. "Metaphors and Values in Higher Education." *Academe,* 1985, *71,* 22–28.

Easter, O. "Septima Poinsette Clark: Unsung Heroine of the Civil Rights Movement." In E. Peterson (ed.), *Freedom Road: Adult Education of African Americans.* Malabar, Fla.: Krieger, 1996.

Essert, P. "The Discussion Group in Adult Education in America." In Mary L. Ely (ed.), *Handbook of Adult Education in the United States.* New York: Teachers College, Columbia University, 1948.

Gabelnick, F., MacGregor, J., Matthews, R., and Smith, B. (eds.). *Learning Communities.* New Directions for Teaching and Learning, no. 41. San Francisco: Jossey-Bass, 1990.

Gratton, C. H. *In Quest of Knowledge: A Historical Perspective on Adult Education.* New York: Association Press, 1955.

Guy, T. "The American Association of Adult Education and the Experiments in African American Adult Education." In E. Peterson (ed.), *Freedom Road: Adult Education of African Americans.* Malabar, Fla.: Krieger, 1996.

Gyant, L. "Alain Leroy Locke: More Than an Adult Educator." In E. Peterson (ed.), *Freedom Road: Adult Education of African Americans.* Malabar, Fla.: Krieger, 1996.

Hart, J. K. *Education in the Humane Community.* New York: HarperCollins, 1951.

Hart, M. "Critical Theory and Beyond: Further Perspectives on Emancipatory Education." *Adult Education Quarterly,* 1990, *40,* 125–138.

Heaney, T. "When Adult Education Stood for Democracy." *Adult Education Quarterly,* 1992, *43,* 51–59.

Heaney, T. *Adult Education for Social Change: From Center Stage to the Wings and Back Again.* Information Series No. 365. Columbus: ERIC Clearinghouse on Adult, Career, and Vocational Education, Center on Education and Training for Employment, College of Education, The Ohio State University, 1996.

Hiemstra, R. *Lifelong Learning: An Exploration of Adult and Continuing Education Within a Setting of Lifelong Learning Needs.* Baldwinsville, N.Y.: HiTree Press, 1984.

Hiemstra, R. *The Educative Community: Linking the Community, Education, and the Family.* Baldwinsville, N.Y.: HiTree Press, 1985.

Horton, M., and Freire, P. *We Make the Road by Walking: Conversations on Education and Social Change.* Philadelphia: Temple University Press, 1990.

Hugo, J. "Perhaps It Is the Person First and the Subject Matter Second: Social Relations and the Construction of Cultural and Civic Curricula in a Women's Study Club, 1885–1985." Unpublished doctoral dissertation, Adult Education Department, Syracuse University, 1996.

Hugo, J. "Creating an Intellectual Basis for Friendship: Practice and Politics in a White Women's Study Group." In V. Sheared and P. Sissel (eds.), *Making Space: Merging Theory and Practice in Adult Education.* New York: Bergin & Garvey, 2001.

Imel, S. *Learning Communities/Communities of Practice.* Trends and Issues Alert, no. 26. Columbus: ERIC Clearinghouse on Adult, Career, and Vocational Education, Center on Education and Training for Employment, College of Education, The Ohio State University, 2001.

Jarvis, P. *The Sociology of Adult and Continuing Education*. London: Croom Helm, 1985.

Kett, J. *The Pursuit of Knowledge Under Difficulties: From Self-Improvement to Adult Education in America, 1750–1990*. Stanford, Calif.: Stanford University Press, 1994.

Knowles, M. *The Modern Practice of Adult Education: From Pedagogy to Andragogy* (rev. ed.). New York: Cambridge University Press, 1980.

Kornbluh, J. L. *A New Deal for Workers' Education: The Workers' Service Program, 1933–1942*. Chicago: University of Illinois Press, 1987.

Kotinsky, R. *Adult Education and the Social Scene*. Englewood Cliffs, N.J.: Appleton-Century-Crofts, 1933.

Lakes, R. *The New Vocationalism: Deweyan, Marxist, and Freirean Themes*. Information Series No. 369. Columbus: ERIC Clearinghouse on Adult, Career, and Vocational Education, Center on Education and Training for Employment, College of Education, The Ohio State University, 1997.

Lindeman, E. *The Meaning of Adult Education*. Montreal: Harvest House, 1961. (Originally published 1926.)

Marsick, V. J., Bitterman, J., and van der Veen, R. *From the Learning Organization to Learning Communities Toward a Learning Society*. Information Series No. 382. Columbus: ERIC Clearinghouse on Adult, Career, and Vocational Education, Center on Education and Training for Employment, College of Education, The Ohio State University, 2000.

Oliver, L. *Study Circles: Coming Together for Personal Growth and Social Change*. Washington, D.C.: Seven Locks Press, 1987.

Palloff, R. M., and Pratt, K. *Building Learning Communities in Cyberspace: Effective Strategies for the On-Line Classroom*. San Francisco: Jossey-Bass, 1999.

Potts, E. "The Du Bois-Washington Debate: Conflicting Strategies." In E. Peterson (ed.), *Freedom Road: Adult Education of African Americans*. Malabar, Fla.: Krieger, 1996.

Podeschi, R. "Philosophies, Practices, and American Values." *Lifelong Learning: An Omnibus of Practice and Research*, 1986, *9*(4), 4–6, 27.

Proctor, R. "Metaphors of Adult Education: Beyond Penance Toward Family." *Adult Education Quarterly*, 1991, *41*, 63–74.

Putnam, R. D. *Bowling Alone: The Collapse and Revival of American Community*. New York: Touchstone, 2001.

Rogers, M. "Autonomous Groups and Adult Education." *Adult Education Journal*, Oct. 1947, pp. 176–179.

Rose, A. D. "Review of *Adult Education in the American Experience: From the Colonial Period to the Present*, by H. Stubblefield and P. Keane." *Adult Education Quarterly*, 1995, *45*, 227–231.

Rose, A. D. "Group Learning in Adult Education: Its Historical Roots." In S. Imel (ed.), *Learning in Groups: Exploring Fundamental Principles, New Uses, and Emerging Opportunities*. New Directions for Adult and Continuing Education, no. 71. San Francisco: Jossey-Bass, 1996.

Schultz, T. W. "Investment in Human Capital." *American Economic Review*, 1961, *1*, 1–17.

Schied, F. M. "Struggling to Learn, Learning to Struggle: Workers, Workplace Learning, and the Emergence of Human Resource Development." In V. Sheared and P. A. Sissel (eds.), *Making Space: Merging Theory and Practice in Adult Education*. New York: Bergin & Garvey, 2001.

Scott, A. F. *Natural Allies: Women's Associations in American History*. Urbana: University of Illinois Press, 1991.

Sklar, K. K. "Two Political Cultures in the Progressive Era: The National Consumers' League and the American Association for Labor Legislation." In L. Kerber, A. Kessler-Harris, and K. Sklar (ed.), *U.S. History as Women's History: New Feminist Essays*. Chapel Hill: University of North Carolina Press, 1995.

St. Clair, R. "On the Commonplace: Reclaiming Community in Adult Education." *Adult Education Quarterly,* 1998, *49*(1), 5–14.

Stein, M. R. *The Eclipse of Community: An Interpretation of American Studies.* Princeton, N.J.: Princeton University Press, 1960.

Stubblefield, H. *Towards a History of Adult Education in America: The Search for a Unifying Principle.* London: Croom Helm, 1988.

Stubblefield, H., and Keane, P. *Adult Education in the American Experience: From the Colonial Period to the Present.* San Francisco: Jossey-Bass, 1994.

Susman, W. *Culture as History: The Transformation of American Society in the Twentieth Century.* New York: Pantheon Books, 1984.

Taylor, R., Rockhill, K., and Fieldhouse, R. *University Adult Education in England and the USA: A Reappraisal of the Liberal Tradition.* London: Croom Helm, 1985.

Wilson, A. L. "Telling Tales Out of School—Whose Story Needs Telling?" *Adult Education Quarterly,* 1995, *45*(4), 240–244.

Zuboff, S. *In the Age of the Smart Machine.* New York: Basic Books, 1988.

JANE M. HUGO is on the national staff of Laubach Literacy in Syracuse, New York.

2

Learning in community means creating local knowledge from aspects of communal life. Through a six-stage process, adult educators can help community members become independent learners and co-creators of community knowledge.

Creating Local Knowledge Through Learning in Community: A Case Study

David S. Stein

Learning in community is an expression of the desire to engage with, learn with, and create local knowledge. Unique features of learning in community are that it is voluntary, members share teaching and learning roles, and it brings about a change in the individual but primarily in relation to the community. Wenger and Snyder (2000) refer to the idea of learning in community as a community of practice. A community of practice is a group of people "informally bound together by shared expertise and passion for a joint enterprise. . . . sharing their experiences and knowledge in free-flowing creative ways that foster new approaches to solving problems" (p. 140). Learning in community is a social practice; a group of people representing the diversity of a community come together to create local knowledge from in-depth study of local situations and put what they learn into practice to bring about a desired future.

This chapter describes how a geographically bounded group can become a community of practice by creating its own local knowledge. My objective is to share some of my insights into the meaning and the practice of learning in community. These thoughts arose from my experiences as a participant-observer working with the citizens of a semiurban county in the Midwest to create a learning community. The ideas expressed are based on my field notes, documents, and conversations with the participants in the project. I was engaged with the community over a period of eighteen months. Buckeye County is a fictitious name used to preserve the site's confidentiality. This chapter presents a case study describing how a community committee—Community Futures 2010—came to take charge of its learning, own its learning, and create its own local knowledge.

NEW DIRECTIONS FOR ADULT AND CONTINUING EDUCATION, no. 95, Fall 2002   © Wiley Periodicals, Inc.

As an adult educator, I am interested in how a community creates local knowledge, shares this knowledge, takes ownership of its issues, builds community capacity to take action on its problems, reflects on that action, and creates knowledge that is useful for sustaining learning in community. *Creating local knowledge* means that citizens who live the situation work in partnership with experts to define problems; collect and interpret data from a community's economic, social, political, and historical context; and intervene in the community's daily life to construct a desirable future (Lacy, 2001). First, I will describe the community to provide historical context for the case. Next, I will discuss the concepts of cooperative inquiry and participation as the guiding premises for moving a group toward learning in community. Third, I will propose a model that describes the stages a group moves through on the way to learning in community. The chapter will conclude with reflections from the field on the connection between learning in community and social change. The chapter will be organized around three questions.

- What does it mean for a community to participate in learning in community?
- How does a community take ownership of its learning?
- How does a community connect its learning to social change?

Description of the Case

Toward the end of the 1990s, the Ohio Department of Health, in coordination with the Ohio Department of Human Services, informed local health departments and other social service agencies that grants would no longer be awarded solely on the basis of state priorities. Applicants would now need to show that funds for services or interventions were based on locally obtained community health assessment data. A proposed project had to link health indicators, health risks, and proposed outcomes from the intervention. This notice stimulated counties to conduct health assessments based on subjective and objective indicators of health. In response to the state mandate, Buckeye County Health Department organized a citizens' group to help establish local health priorities and health interventions. Buckeye County is a semiurban county of approximately fifty thousand citizens. Although still mostly agricultural, the county is being transformed into an industrial center outside a major metropolitan area. The health department has been very active in forming community coalitions to address individual health issues, such as teenage pregnancy, nutrition, and childhood immunizations. The citizens' community group, which was named Health Watch 2000, was charged with the responsibility to create a community health plan and establish priorities and community health programs. However, Health Watch 2000 failed to take concerted action to improve health in the community. Momentum for community learning and action was lost because there was little citizen involvement. The best that a small group made up of members of the institutional sector of the community (health department, county extension, Head Start, and local hospital personnel) was able to do was begin a directory of services. A member of Health Watch 2000 noted that the spirit of the community for the action was gone. However, the idea of the group did seem to resonate with an interest in a wider notion of community and the meaning of quality of life in that community. One member of Health Watch 2000, who attended a workshop on community asset building (Kretzmann and McKnight, 1993), expressed the idea that quality of life could be extended to embrace the entire community system rather than just be concerned with health needs.

The idea of a learning community emerged as the focus for a community investigation. A thriving learning community continually creates and improves the physical and social environment and expands those community resources that enable people to help each other perform all the functions of life and develop their highest potential. A thriving learning community recognizes the community's responsibility to embrace access to high-quality lifelong education, affordable and adequate housing, safe places for recreation and religious and cultural expression, and jobs that inspire and pay a livable wage (Duhl, 1990; Longworth, 1999). A thriving learning community honors diversity and provides meaningful opportunities for volunteerism and civic engagement (Johnson, Grossman, and Cassidy, 1996).

Helping this community to learn about its desired quality of life and become a thriving learning community was the guiding vision for my involvement in this case. Thus, I would become involved with various public, private, educational, religious, and agricultural sectors of the community, as well as with just ordinary folk. A new group, Community Futures 2010, would need to be formed. To create Community Futures 2010, representatives from the health, human services, political (townships and villages), educational, farming, industrial, welfare, religious, and legal communities were invited to participate in a sustained community effort to learn about the issues affecting the lives and future of county residents. How the Community Futures 2010 committee learned in community to create its own local knowledge and used that knowledge to build a thriving learning community is the focus of this chapter.

What Does It Mean for a Community to Participate in Learning in Community?

Cooperative inquiry (Heron, 1996) and participation (Reason, 1994) served as the conceptual bases for this inquiry. The defining characteristics of cooperative inquiry are that adult educators and citizen learners decide together on the research questions, method of inquiry, and interpretation of data; are immersed in the experience; and create shared meaning from that experience. The adult educator, also learning in community, involves the community in designing a framework for investigating the issues that are important to it and on which it will take action. The community thus learns through practice how to define a problem, study a problem, collect and interpret data on a problem, and act on the problem (Elden, 1981). The essence of learning in community is that the participants are the subjects of study, the researchers, and the learners; their roles and their experience form the basis for learning.

Reason (1994) argues that the sharing of experience and interpretation is the means by which learning occurs. Experience and reflection on that experience serve as the stimulus for learners to connect learning to action. Learning and action are related to the interpretations of the data that the participants collect. Notice that the emphasis is on engagement with a situation rather than on listening to reports of activities conducted by experts. To learn in community means that members conduct the inquiry and generate their own local knowledge and ways of knowing. The members must have a say in the conduct of the inquiry. In Buckeye County, the citizens inquired about how to realize a desired future for their community.

Learning in community is based on the notion of true participation, where learners take responsibility for the search for knowledge and create their own meaning based on their interactions in the real world. Reason (1994) asserts that true participation is essential for local knowledge generation and ownership.

People have a right to participate in decisions about the design of research (including its management and conclusions drawn from it) whose purpose is to formulate knowledge about them. With cooperative inquiry, they are not disempowered, oppressed, or misrepresented by the researcher's values. To generate knowledge about people without their full participation in deciding how to do so is to misrepresent their personhood and neglect their capacity for action (Reason, 1994).

I found the participation concept to be powerful and practical in bringing about sustained community learning. Participation becomes a conceptual tool for understanding learning in community and for a community to learn how to engage in learning. Without participation—that is, active involvement and ownership of the learning—action on that learning would not happen. Participation becomes the framework for building learning in community.

Participation means becoming engaged with others and generating the situations to be researched. It means the inquirers create their own meaning and take actions based on data generated by and from them in a particular context. Participation, in a community learning sense, is based on a set of assumptions:

- Experts are not the only ones capable of producing valid, useful knowledge. Ordinary people can do so too. Knowledge has a cultural and historical component that only the community can fully appreciate (Reason, 1994).

- Participation creates a sense of ownership in the project and its outcomes, ownership by those who will live with those outcomes. Experts can leave the situation, but the participants must remain.
- Participation is knowing about the situation and being able to create courses of action that are relevant. The feeling is that participation in the inquiry will lead to some change (Cosier and Glennie, 1994).
- Participation is fundamental to building community capacity for change and for sustaining that change.
- Participation means honoring the contributions of those who attend meetings, being involved in defining and resolving needs, and including diverse viewpoints and interests that come together for collective action (Goodman and others, 1998).

Participation reduces the distance between the ordinary people who have to live the change and the experts who create it. The community owns the ideas and actions for change. Change is achieved from shared learning rather than engineered by theoretical or expert knowledge. The adult educator might begin but does not control the process of change.

How Does a Community Take Ownership of Its Learning?

In addition to guiding the processes used to promote learning in community, the concepts of participation and cooperative inquiry provided the theoretical and conceptual bases for the Six C model of learning in community. The Six C model describes the process a group moves through in learning to learn in community. It is not a linear process. Instead, the community cycles back and forth through the six stages. In *committing,* participants identify an issue of concern. During *contracting,* they take responsibility for studying the issue. In *campaigning,* they engage with data. When they *contribute,* they take actions related to meaning making and reflecting on action. When they *communicate,* they share insights with the group and the community at large. In *continuing,* the final stage, they plan for future action-reflection cycles, including charting additional needs, reviewing new data, evaluating the success of the actions they have taken, and posing problems. Then they transmit this collective knowledge to new members. These stages are based on my observations and reflections on group activities and my work with community health assessments (Stanley and Stein, 1998). The model illustrates that the adult educator may assist in the process but not control the direction or depth of change taking place in the group. The following paragraphs describe each stage in detail.

Committing. Committing is the stage in which the structure is organized, norms for participation are established, participants are recruited, and the inquiry is initiated. To learn in community, the community should to the extent possible represent the whole system. Commitment begins when a group takes ownership of its learning. In Buckeye County, commitment began when representatives from the health department, the county extension, Head Start, and the local hospital invited me to talk with them about organizing a communitywide discussion on a healthy community. The representatives from these agencies would become the steering committee of Community Futures 2010 and would provide the overall coordination for the process. The steering committee was not a decision-making body but instead took the responsibility to form and convene the Community Futures 2010 group. I explained that my role would be to mirror, to reflect, and at times to question the group process. I would not interpret data but would lead discussions about data. I would not make recommendations but would help the group collect, analyze, and interpret data. Once in this role, I had to deal with ongoing tensions as the Community Futures 2010 committee struggled with independence as learners and dependence on me, the adult educator, to provide the answers.

The steering committee and I agreed to blend our insider and outsider knowledge to form an academic-practitioner team. Attributes that have been identified as essential for a functioning academic-community team include good reasons to work together, previous acquaintance with each other, a formal structure, respect and willingness to share authority and power, complementary strengths, and experience in each other's environments (Barber, 2000; Heitmann and Selle, 2000; Camino and Heidrich, 2000).

As an outsider, I needed to engage with the community to learn the history, values, and culture so I could assist the group in learning about its capacity to bring about change. However, in such cases experts do not lead but transfer their technical knowledge to the community (Baker and Teaser-Polk, 1998). They provide access to information to improve the collective intelligence of the community. They build on the skills, wisdom, and collective experience of the group (Weisbord and Janoff, 1995). Thus, I attended steering committee meetings, observed the functioning of existing community coalitions, read documents of previous attempts to address quality-of-life concerns, attended community celebrations, and talked with citizens about everyday life in Buckeye County.

To enhance the possibilities for learning, I stressed dialogic models for interaction and norms for interaction. Being mutually respectful and valuing disagreement, allowing equal voice regardless of institutional or social position, and listening to the data and each other were operating principles for the committee's functioning and deliberations (Sullivan, Kone, Senturia, Chrisman, Ciske, and Krieger, 2001). To learn in community, structural and interpersonal supports must be put in place and monitored by the group and the adult educator. The steering committee agreed with the principles and hosted a communitywide workshop as a means to recruit participants.

In February 1998, approximately sixty community representatives from the health, human services, political (townships and villages), educational, agricultural, industrial, welfare, religious, and legal community sectors were invited to attend a half-day workshop on images of the future for Buckeye County. Using the *future search methodology* (Weisbord and Janoff, 1995), participants would investigate their experiences as residents in the county and come to common ground on those elements that would be desirable to make the county a better place to live. The search for common ground is the discovery of shared intentions and the commitment to take responsibility for the outcomes of a community project. The future search method is based on the assumption that experts do not solve problems; rather, it is the people who live in the community and who learn to view the community as a system who have the collective wisdom and skill to work together to improve the quality of life. Thus, the inquirers learn more about their viewpoints and the viewpoints of others. When common ground is explored, creative energy is released through the shared learning. Projects can be undertaken using the common skills and wisdom acquired by the community. People simultaneously discover mutual values, innovative ideas, commitment, and support. The primary notion is that by charting common ground participants take personal responsibility to bring about change.

The outcome of the workshop was a set of scenarios describing the future quality of life in Buckeye County. Participants made a commitment to learn about their community through focus groups and sustained engagement with the data and with each other.

Focus groups would be used to give voice to ordinary citizens and to compare the Community Futures 2010 group's views with the views of everyday citizens. The Community Futures 2010 group embarked on a set of activities to study the issues, thoughts, and feelings of the community related to bringing about possible futures. The local newspaper expressed the desire for the whole community to engage in learning about its future.

It takes a whole community to make an effort like this. What some considered to be assets of the county, others thought needed improvement. Similarly, some felt that the issues should be tackled at the community level and then narrowed to individual groups, whereas others believed in starting with the families and children and working outward to the communities (Fout, 1998a).

Contracting. In the contracting stage community members accept responsibility for posing questions, collecting data, and negotiating meaning from the data. Contracting refers to a set of activities that prepare the community to learn. Community members agree to be open to alternative ways of thinking, seeing, and experiencing everyday life. Volunteers were recruited from the Community Futures 2010 committee to serve as focus group moderators, attend moderator training, and organize focus groups in eighteen townships. I agreed to serve as recorder for the focus groups, do the transcription, and organize the data for analysis. However, the interpretation of the data and the actions that might follow were tasks for the committee members. Contracting developed further as the entire committee organized into task forces to explore specific themes identified from the data collected. Session participants agreed to become involved in collecting data—conducting focus groups, analyzing the data, and taking action based on the data. During this stage, participants learned about the power of ordinary voices and how to engage an entire community in learning about their quality of life.

Campaigning. Campaigning describes the manner in which participants are immersed in gathering the data and experience firsthand how they can take responsibility for learning about the issues in their community. Three data collection techniques were used here: focus groups, telephone interviews, and school-administered surveys. All tools were developed by me with input from the steering committee and approval from the entire Community Futures 2010 committee.

Focus groups were conducted in eighteen townships; approximately 120 people were involved. Meetings were held in high schools, churches, town halls, homes, and community halls. Focus groups were held with low-income families, high school students, and direct providers of social services. A unique feature of the focus groups was that each was conducted by a member of the inquiry group and organized by a local resident in that village. Transcripts produced from tapes were checked for accuracy with the focus group moderator-convener.

The telephone survey of randomly selected adults was conducted by the health department using students from the state university to make the calls; the goal was to extend a voice to those not included in the focus groups. The in-class survey of middle and high school students was conducted by district school nurses. The university's resources were used to code, tabulate, and organize the data. Interpreting the data and its importance to the community was the responsibility of Community Futures 2010.

During the contracting stage, the committee learned how to plan and conduct a field research project. Members served as focus group facilitators. They learned how to withhold judgments as other citizens commented on services provided by community agencies such as the health department or the library. Community Futures 2010 members developed skills in data collection. In addition, learning to listen to the voices of ordinary citizens was an enlightening experience for participants.

Contributing. Contributing is the stage in which each member of the learning team becomes an active agent in interpreting the data and creating shared meaning. Community Futures 2010 compared the perspectives of community leaders, social service agency personnel serving the community, and citizens of the townships. They interpreted the findings from the focus groups reports and negotiated among the various images of the future. Organized into teams, they created action plans to address concerns based on their interpretation of the data. In this stage, learning connects to action.

Five teams were organized around the following themes, which emerged from focus group data: land use and uncontrolled growth, youth and recreation, improvements in education, better business and industry growth in the county, and improved health. Teams created their own meeting schedules and agreed to share their learning with the other teams. At this point the group's dependence on the facilitator lessened. The group realized its ability to use data—to use data as a way to gain insights into the community and to use data as a tool for taking action. A task force member commented to the local paper on the importance of learning in community.

The real plus of this assessment phase was the ownership that residents in each of the townships felt. They really had an interest in taking steps to improve the county. Armed with the knowledge of what community members really wanted and what they were currently faced with, agency leaders and local government officials had to put a plan into action. Participants in this study would continue to analyze the data that were collected. As their work progressed, efforts would be made to reach the ultimate goal of providing a better place to live in the year 2010 (Fout, 1998b).

Communicating. The communication stage describes the processes and activities used to disseminate and share the learning gained. In this case, the task forces provided updates on their progress and the issues to the entire Community Futures 2010 group and the whole community. Kegler (Kegler, Steckler, McLeroy, and Malek, 1998) offers insight into some of the factors that sustain and increase the effectiveness of community coalitions, which by analogy, are learning groups. Quality of communication was the only operational process that correlated with member participation, member satisfaction, extent of plan implemented, and number of activities accomplished by a coalition. Thus, there is a need not only for communication with the community at large but also for communication within the group in order to build trust, a sense of belonging, and a focus at each meeting.

To further communication both within the group and with the community, the steering committee coordinated the meeting schedule, distributed minutes, and sent reminders of meetings. Each task force prepared a report to the community by selecting the appropriate parts from the data analysis report and their own activities plan. The group wrote a collaborative community report and decided to distribute the findings through the local media to the public. An excerpt from the group's March 1999 minutes shows how the committee deliberated on its responsibility to keep the community informed of the project: "The next step will be to compile a summary of findings for distribution throughout the community. Several questions still need to be addressed: Should a subcommittee be formed to look at the data and prepare an executive summary? How much information should be shared with the public? How will the focus group participants be included? Should the summary include highlights on the greatest risk factors? Should the school information be aggregated? (The response was yes.) Should representatives of all subcommittees be included in the committee looking at the data? (Again, the response was yes.) RM and DR agree to co-chair the data review committee to prepare a document for public distribution."

Minutes of the September 10, 1999, committee meeting recorded a decision to make subcommittees responsible for updating the public through a series of local newspaper articles and providing the community with access to data. The minutes further stated that the subcommittees had the responsibility to keep the community informed about current topics and actions taken. The minutes also suggested that the committee could become a communitywide "information clearinghouse" and "communication headquarters for current projects."

As the five task forces shared insights with each other and the entire community, citizens could begin to see how the interrelationships of all the community's subsystems affected the county's quality of life. The community began to learn about the connections between access to health, job opportunities, economic development, and overall quality of life.

Continuing. Continuity refers to the stage in which a group takes actions to sustain and continue the learning. In this stage, Community Futures 2010 practiced reflection on action and generated new issues to investigate.

Continuity occurs through regularly scheduled meetings, celebrations, and entry of new members. In this case, quarterly meetings were held to report on progress and continue the reflection on action. They were used to update committee members on actions taken in the five focus areas of business, education, land use, recreation, and health. Through the quarterly meetings, a new learning cycle could begin and the spirit of collaboration and learning could be continued. A committee member who was interviewed by the local newspaper highlighted the importance of the quarterly meetings in maintaining the momentum for learning.

We were fortunate in Buckeye County because the different agencies collaborated well. Several agencies collaborated on the community assessment. It would require the assistance of everyone involved to ensure that the community saw results from the project. The important thing was not to let it fail; it had to be an ongoing effort. It was decided that the group would evaluate to see if the intervention was doing what was intended. If not, they would decide if they needed to redirect their efforts (Fout, 1998c).

As of the writing of this chapter, the quarterly meetings have been ongoing since February 1998. The Community Futures 2010 group has welcomed new members, celebrated accomplishments, honored departing members. Although the membership changes, the collective and collected wisdom of the group remains. The group continues to learn and to be involved in creating the future of its community. The December 8, 2000, quarterly meeting minutes indicated that twenty-five community organizations were represented at the end-of-year celebration. By comparison, the December 10, 1999, minutes indicated that only fifteen community organizations participated. The learning continues independent of the particular members who continually enter and exit the group. Continuity is preserved through the meetings and the commitment of the group to continue to learn.

How Does a Community Connect Its Learning to Social Change?

This community's learning resulted in positive change. A teen health coalition has been formed to investigate teen and school-related health issues further; the teen group has received state grants to conduct asset-building projects in the schools. The education group formed partnerships with the sheriff and other social agencies to create a safer school environment. A deputy sheriff visits all county high schools and middle schools to curb school violence, and according to the minutes of the December 10, 2000, meeting, "received good reception by school administrators and students." In addition, the education group is active in conducting training and involving schools, churches, youth-serving organizations, and business and government organizations in promoting community asset building. The library board conducted interviews with community residents to determine the feasibility of establishing a new library and balancing the needs of book readers with Internet and technological resources. The business group hired an economic development director and has conducted microenterprise training for county residents whose household income is up to 300 percent of the poverty level and with a baby in the home. The recreation group has appropriated and remodeled a vacant building. The land use group was involved in securing a farmland preservation education grant. A representative of Community Futures 2010 serves on the farmland preservation task force.

These actions were informed by the data collected by Community Futures 2010 and the discussions with the county's residents about its future growth and development. The learning taking place includes knowledge and skill in building citizen participation, gaining a sense of community, and discussing and coming to understand community history and values, especially ties to the land and the interconnectedness of the citizens of the community.

Although the main effort was to learn, the process also developed community capacity. *Community capacity* may be defined as the strengths and resources a community applies toward building a healthier community (Kreuter, Lezin, and Young, 2000). In this case, the community learned about its assets and it can now build on these assets. Change is occurring in Buckeye County. However, the change is accomplished within existing community structures, and at this time has not yet involved the social, gender, economic, or the other inequalities that may be the root causes of the issues. This may change as the community's confidence in its learning and ability to engage in community inquiry increases.

Conclusion

This case shows how a geographically bounded community can develop the capacity to learn in community. It illustrates that learning in community involves a series of stages in which a group engages in a social process leading to the development of collective learning. The learning is based on encounters with everyday, meaningful situations. It is the situations and the interactions with others that serve as the textbook for learning. To learn in community, members create local knowledge and apply that knowledge to address issues of importance to them. The intent is to sustain the learning and build the capacity for future collective learning rather than simply seek a solution to a problem. Although a desire to solve problems certainly motivates a group to engage in learning, this case shows how a community group voluntarily engages in a long-term process of reflecting on community issues from historical, cultural, and social perspectives. In addition to learning how to act on community problems, the group described here learned how to develop relationships to sustain their learning, take responsibility to act on the learning, and respect the experiences of all group members involved in generating the learning. The social interaction is the mechanism by which the group developed collective learning. Thus, although members may enter and exit the group, collective learning continues throughout the group's existence.

The engagement of Community Futures 2010 with learning in community represents the notion of an active civil society. Fryer (1999), while tracing the development of self-directed work and community groups, calls local engagement a hallmark of lifelong learning.

Today, active citizenship is manifest in the contribution being made by local communities to their own social and economic regeneration. Local engagement means that people define their own needs and identify their own priorities. Such activity connects with people's own priorities, builds their confidence and self-esteem, and gives them a practical sense of achievement. Learning can undoubtedly help greatly with these objectives (Fryer, 1999).

Learning in community is marked by a community creating and perpetuating a participative collaborative of organizations and persons investing time and resources to inquire ever more deeply into their culture, values, and needs. Learning in community creates a collective described by Longworth (1999) as an entity that "mobilizes all its resources in every sector to develop and enrich all its human potential for the fostering of personal growth, the maintenance of social cohesion, and the creation of prosperity" (p. 109).

The meaning of learning community lies in the increasing confidence of a group that its ability to learn and to act on that learning resides in the group itself, and that the learning it creates can encompass the whole community.

References

Baker, E., and Teaser-Polk, C. "Measuring Community Capacity: Where Do We Go From Here?" *Health Education and Behavior,* 1998, *25,* 279–283.

Barber, P. "Extending the Learning Community." Paper presented at the 29th Annual Conference of the Association for Research on Nonprofit Organizations and Voluntary Action. New Orleans, Nov. 16–18, 2000.

Camino, L., and Heidrich, K. "Voices of Wisdom: Knowledge and Experience from Practitioner-Academic Teams in the Building Bridges Initiative." Paper presented at the 29th Annual Conference of the Association for Research on Nonprofit Organizations and Voluntary Action, New Orleans, Nov. 16–18, 2000.

Cosier, J., and Glennie, S. "Supervising the Child Protection Process: A Multidisciplinary Inquiry." In P. Reason (ed.), *Participation in Human Inquiry.* Thousand Oaks, Calif.: Sage, 1994.

Duhl, H. *The Social Entrepreneurship of Change.* New York: Pace University Press, 1990.

Elden, M. "Sharing the Research Work: Participative Research and Its Role Demands." In P. Reason and J. Rowan (eds.), *Human Inquiry: A Sourcebook of New Paradigm Research.* New York: Wiley, 1981.

Fout, S. "Workshop Attendees Focus on Buckeye County 2010." *Herald,* Feb. 27, 1998a, p. 1.

Fout, S. "Study Group Reports on County's Future." *Herald,* Dec. 14, 1998b, pp. 1, 3.

Fout, S. "County Assessment Survey Under Way." *Herald,* Oct. 7, 1998c, pp. 1, 3.

Fryer, H. "Creating Learning Cultures: Next Steps in Achieving the Learning Age." Second Report of the National Advisory Group for Continuing Education and Lifelong Learning. Sheffield, England: NAGCELL, 1999.

Goodman, R., and others, "Identifying and Defining the Dimensions of Community Capacity to Provide a Basis for Measurement." *Health Education and Behavior,* 1998, *25,* 258–278.

Heitmann, J., and Selle, P. "Practitioner and Scholar: Mutual Advantage." Bergen, Norway: Norway Research Center in Organization and Management, 2000.

Heron, J. *Cooperative Inquiry: Research into the Human Condition.* Thousand Oaks, Calif.: Sage, 1996.

Johnson, K., Grossman, W., and Cassidy, A. *Collaborating to Improve Community Health.* San Francisco: Jossey-Bass, 1996.

Kegler, M., Steckler, A., McLeroy, K., and Malek, S. "Factors That Contribute to Effective Community Health Promotion Coalitions: A Study of Ten Project ASSIST Coalitions in North Carolina." *Health Education and Behavior,* 1998, *25*(3), 338–353.

Kretzmann, J., and McKnight, J. *Building Communities from the Inside Out: A Path Toward Finding and Mobilizing a Community's Assets.* Chicago: ACTA, 1993.

Kreuter, M., Lezin, N., and Young, L. "Evaluating Community-Based Collaborative Mechanisms: Implications for Practitioners." *Health Promotion Practice,* 2000, *1,* 49–63.

Lacy, W. "Democratizing Science in an Era of Expert and Private Knowledge." *Higher Education Exchange,* 2001, *1,* 52–61.

Longworth, N. *Making Lifelong Learning Work: Learning Cities for a Learning Century.* London: Kogan Page, 1999.

Reason, P. *Participation in Human Inquiry.* Thousand Oaks, Calif.: Sage, 1994.

Stanley, S., and Stein, D. "Health Watch 2000: Community Health Assessment in South Central Ohio." *Journal of Community Health Nursing,* 1998, *15*(4), 225–236.

Sullivan, M., and others, "Researcher and Researched-Community Perspectives: Toward Bridging the Gap." *Health Education & Behavior,* 2001, *28*(2), 130–149.

Weisbord, M., and Janoff, S. *Future Search: An Action Guide to Finding Common Ground in Organizations and Communities.* San Francisco: Berrett-Koehler, 1995.

Wenger, E., and Snyder, W. "Communities of Practice: The Organizational Frontier." *Harvard Business Review,* Jan.-Feb. 2000, pp. 139–145.

DAVID S. STEIN is associate professor of adult education and workforce development at The Ohio State University, College of Education.

3

In Ohio's For the Common Good project, learning played a key role in the development and implementation of interagency linkage teams. Adult educators can assist in developing successful collaborative partnerships by making the role of learning more explicit.

For the Common Good: Learning Through Interagency Collaboration

Susan Imel, Cynthia J. Zengler

Adult educators frequently work with collaborative partnerships and may be expected to facilitate the development of collaborative linkages. Although the process of collaboration has been studied (for example, Mattessich and Monsey, 1992; Wood and Gray, 1991), the connection between collaboration and learning remains relatively unexplored. What role, if any, does learning play in a successful collaboration? Does the process of collaboration lead to the development of learning communities? These questions and others have not been addressed either in the literature on collaboration or in adult education. Based on the experiences of Ohio's For the Common Good project, this chapter examines the connection between collaborative groups and learning. First, an overview of the project is provided; this is followed by a discussion of the elements of successful collaboration. The role of learning in local linkage teams formed through the Common Good is explored next. Finally, a fourth section connects the learning that occurred with theories of adult learning.

For the Common Good

For the Common Good is an Ohio project whose goal is to facilitate the formation of local interagency linkage teams throughout the state. Local teams, whose members represent a variety of community agencies, focus on improving services to at-risk youth and adults through the development of collaborative interagency linkages. Initiated in 1990 as a result of the Family Support Act of 1988, the project has expanded its focus to all workforce development efforts and operates under the direction of a team composed of state-level staff.

Established as a means to address a specific legislative initiative, For the Common Good has also responded to the national trend of collaborative linkages as a strategy for implementing systemic change. In Ohio, as in other states, the reality of welfare reform and other initiatives, such as one-stop systems, reinforce collaboration as a process to facilitate making quality services available to families and communities. Most of the initial one-stop systems funded in Ohio had Common Good roots; that is, a Common Good local linkage team formed the nucleus for the development of the collaboration. Under the Workforce Investment Act (WIA) of 1998, Common Good teams continue to play key roles in the further development of the local collaboration required by that legislation.

Like many other good ideas, successful local interagency collaboration is not easily achieved. It takes time, energy, leadership, and commitment on the part of the agencies involved. Despite these challenges, approximately half of the forty-seven Common Good local linkage teams (LLTs) formed through the project have remained active in some form, and many have made remarkable progress in developing integrated services with a customer-centered focus. Three follow-up surveys on the LLTs (Imel, 1992, 1994, 1997) provided some information about what factors contributed to their success, but the amount and kind of information that can be collected through follow-up surveys is limited.

To understand more fully what factors lead to successful collaboration at the local level, case studies of five Common Good local linkage teams were conducted (Imel and Zengler, 1999). Later, the role of learning in the development of successful collaboration was explored through a questionnaire mailed to members of the five teams and follow-up telephone interviews with selected individuals (Imel and Zengler, 2000).

Collaboration: The Elements of Success

The experiences of the For the Common Good project demonstrated that local linkage teams "can't be turned out like widgets" (Schorr, 1997, p. 28). Variations in local community contexts, the personalities of individuals on the team, and other factors have meant that each team has had to "reinvent parts of the wheel" in terms of developing successful interagency collaboration (Schorr, 1997, p. 28). In addition, some teams floundered and dissolved, whereas others flourished. To understand what factors contributed to the success of local linkage teams in sustaining collaboration, five teams were studied using a combination of site visits and written documentation.

The following elements were identified as important in the Common Good teams studied. Although the five teams possessed these characteristics to varying degrees (and all teams did not possess every characteristic listed), these characteristics nevertheless seemed to be the essence of successful Common Good LLTs.

Regular Communication. Regular and frequent communication sets the stage for successful collaboration. Members of more than one team mentioned that it was not unusual for them to be in daily contact with one or more Common Good team members.

Customer-Centered Focus. Working jointly to provide better service for common customers was perceived to be the primary purpose of Common Good teams.

Shared Leadership. In terms of leadership, most teams were more like a jazz ensemble than an orchestra. Leadership tended to emerge based on individual talent and interest in a particular activity. Leadership shifted among the members of most teams studied when different individuals assumed leadership responsibility for activities and for the team itself.

Structure and Focus. A plan provided structure and focus for team activities. For most teams studied, projects and activities were an important part of the plan.

Esprit de Corps. Respect for one another and commitment to the Common Good team was evident.

Relationship to One-Stop System. Teams expressed varying relationships to the one-stop center in their areas. On the most successful teams, agency representation was broader than on the one-stop centers in their areas, and the teams perceived their mission as transcending the one-stop system. That is, they saw their mission to be more than that required. Others, however, were struggling to develop a niche for Common Good in light of one-stop implementation.

Support from the Common Good State Team. Initial and continuing support from the state team was important to all teams studied. Most mentioned the gift of uninterrupted time during workshops planned by the state team that allowed them to develop action plans.

Through a review of the literature, Mattessich and Monsey (1992) identified six categories of factors influencing the success of collaboration: environment, membership, process-structure, communication, purpose, and resources. These factors are similar to the ones identified through the study of Common Good LLTs, but they are broader. The category of environment, for example, would encompass the element "relationship to one-stop system" identified in the study of LLTs. During the summer of 1999, when the five Common Good LLTs were visited, the development of the one-stop system as a part of the Workforce Investment Act was a significant environmental factor influencing the local teams.

The process of collaboration in the five LLTs also appeared to be similar to that described in other literature on collaboration (Wood and Gray, 1991). As a part of their efforts to develop a comprehensive theory of collaboration, Wood and Gray said that "collaboration occurs when a group of autonomous stakeholders of a problem domain engage in an interactive process, using shared rules, norms, and structures, to act or decide on issues related to the domain" (p. 146). All LLTs included representatives from distinct agencies or organizations (autonomous stakeholders); the five studied focused on workforce development (problem domain) and had a structure and focus that enabled them to address issues or problems related to workforce development.

Each team that participated in the study was unique. Factors such as community context, personalities of team members, importance placed on interagency collaboration, and so forth contributed to this uniqueness. Yet, the study revealed that the teams shared some elements that contributed to their success in developing and sustaining successful interagency linkages. Teams used "intelligence, experience, and wisdom to sort out [what needs to be done locally to craft the Common Good model] to fit local needs and strengths" (Schorr, 1997, p. 60). The factors identified in the study of the LLTs are similar to those found in the literature (Mattessich and Monsey, 1992), and the process of collaboration is consistent with that identified by Wood and Gray (1991).

The Learning Connection

The role of learning in collaboration did not emerge during the case study phase of the project. Although it appeared that learning had supported the accomplishments of the teams and their members, its part was tacit. To explore the connection between learning and collaboration, therefore, a questionnaire was sent to members of the five teams included in the case study. The questionnaire was designed to discover the role of learning in the success of the Common Good team, the character of the learning, and the types of learning activities in which the team engaged. Follow-up telephone calls were made to some team members to collect additional information.

When asked to describe the role of learning in the success of their Common Good team, 44 percent of the respondents indicted it was "critical" and 56 percent said it was "important." Most—82 percent—characterized the learning that took place as "both individual and group."

The teams engaged in learning activities that included learning how to work together and learning to accomplish specific objectives.

Learning how to work together involved getting to know other members of the team on both a professional and personal level. Team members described this type of learning as follows:

- Getting acquainted with team and others in community, developing a common mission.
- Getting to know (each other); becoming comfortable, familiar, and developing the trust we enjoyed were inherent to our success.

- Information sharing and learning about team members both professionally and personally.

Learning that occurred in order to accomplish specific objectives was also important. Teams engaged in projects and activities such as job fairs, job-readiness workshops, and legislative forums. One team incorporated as a nonprofit organization so that it could serve as its own fiscal agent and apply for grants.

Both kinds of learning were important. According to one team coordinator, the learning about each other helped lay the foundation for the team to accomplish four major goals: creating a clothes closet, providing transportation for common customers, establishing a dental clinic, and mentoring customers. Different members of the team with expertise in an area took the lead and did the research needed to reach the goal. Leadership for the clothes closet was provided by a team member with a background in home economics, and a team member from the department of transportation headed up the transportation area. This team learned from other communities about dental clinics and mentoring; community groups that had experienced success with similar programs visited the team.

Much of the learning reported by the team members might be characterized as *sharing knowledge.* "Sharing knowledge occurs when people are genuinely interested in helping one another develop new capacities for action; it is about creating learning processes" (Senge, 1998, p. 11). The learning about each other set the foundation for teams to engage in the learning required for action. How the learning that occurred in the process of interagency collaboration connects to learning theory is explored in the next section.

Connecting Practice to Theory

Although learning was not mentioned during the visits to the teams, the second phase of the study revealed that, for the individuals surveyed, learning was either critical or important to their team's success. What is the relationship between learning theory and the learning reported by team members? The learning appears to be constructivist in nature with connections to communities of practice and learning communities.

Much of the learning reported by linkage team members can be characterized as *constructivist.* According to constructivist learning theory, individuals actively construct meaning by interacting with their environment and incorporating new information into their existing knowledge (Feden, 1994). Through learning that is constructivist in nature, individuals make sense of their experience (Merriam and Caffarella, 1999).

Constructivist learning theory is congruent with much of adult learning, including self-direction, transformative learning, and situated cognition.

In self-directed learning, individuals engage in active, individual, independent inquiry; these are also characteristics of constructivist learning. Making meaning of both personal and social experience is at the heart of transformative learning. Situated cognition includes concepts such as cognitive apprenticeships with an emphasis on teaching learners different ways of thinking about what they are learning, situated learning, reflective practice, and communities of practice (Merriam and Caffarella, 1999).

Most of the individuals contacted in the follow-up telephone survey indicated that the information about team members and their agencies was instrumental in the work the team was able to do. In other words, they incorporated it into their existing knowledge and moved forward to action. The learning was also self-directed in nature because many of the projects undertaken by the teams involved new learning, and the members had to direct the learning involved in figuring out what to do. It was also related to the area of situated cognition as described in the next section on communities of practice.

Communities of Practice. The term *communities of practice* refers to a group of people who by working together learn by doing and also develop a shared sense of what needs to happen to get a task accomplished (Stamps, 1997; Wenger, 1998). The theory underlying communities of practice is a social learning theory developed by Etienne Wenger (1998) with roots in constructivist learning theory (Merriam and Caffarella, 1999). It places learning in the context of the lived experiences of participation in the world: learning is as much a part of human nature as eating or sleeping, and individuals are quite good at it. The theory is based on four major assumptions: humans are social beings, and this characteristic is a central part of their learning; knowledge is a matter of competence with respect to valued activities; knowing comes from active engagement with these activities; and meaning, the ability to experience the world and engage with it, is the ultimate product of learning (Wenger, 1998).

Communities of practice are informal and often invisible. They form of their own accord through the need to solve common problems and a desire of members to learn from one another. Face-to-face contact is a necessary condition for the collaboration that occurs in communities of practice. In organizations, communities of practice cannot be mandated by management, and they are easy to destroy by meddling (Stamps, 1997).

Some of the Common Good LLTs function as communities of practice. In these teams, learning occurs through active participation in the team—that is, through "being active participants in the practices of social communities" (Wenger, 1998, p. 7). The linkage teams exist for the purpose of developing the capacity of the team members' agencies to serve customers through the development and exchange of knowledge, and the members share a commitment and identification with the group's expertise (Wenger and Snyder, 2000). In addition, the teams have formed voluntarily, and they do not operate under a legislative mandate. The state team has provided support but has allowed them to operate autonomously (Imel and Zengler, 1999).

Learning Organizations. When learning is considered an element of collaboration, most of the Common Good local linkage teams studied also have similarities with learning organizations. In defining a learning organization, Senge stated that "at the elementary level, a learning organization is still a group of people working together to collectively enhance their capacities to create results that they truly care about" (Fulmer and Keys, 1998, p. 33). In this definition, *Common Good local linkage team* could be substituted for the term *learning organization;* it would apply to many of the teams.

In learning organizations, learning occurs at both the individual and team level (Watkins and Marsick, 1993, 1999). Individual learning occurs when people make meaning of their experiences and are then provided an opportunity by the organization to build their knowledge and skills. In team learning, groups of people work and learn collaboratively and create new knowledge as well as the capacity for collaborative action (Watkins and Marsick, 1999).

Significant learning experienced either as an individual or as a part of the team included both learning to work together and learning to accomplish specific activities. The following comments from team members illustrate what some considered to be significant learning:

- I believe we were able to establish a vision to work together to improve our own agencies and how they interacted with other agencies.
- Learning to work together for the job fair and the monthly information from other team members about their agencies' programs were significant.
- Social service agencies are experiencing significant rapid change and the opportunity to normalize what is important.
- Collaboration cannot be mandated from above. It must happen at the individual level. The "coming together" may be mandated but the collaboration is a result of the willingness of the individual personalities to share and trust.
- Learning the evolution of real collaboration was significant, including learning that it takes commitment to work together to make it work.

Several of the Common Good linkage team members reported experiences with learning that reflect the type of learning described by Watkins and Marsick (1993, 1999). One individual, who worked on the development of the clothes closet, said that for her the learning was more personal (that is, individual) than group in nature. The chance to be on the team exposed her to new ideas and created new opportunities for her in the community. However, she also worked with a group of people on the linkage team to make the clothes closet a reality, and the team learning continues about how to accomplish new challenges such as finding a new location and acquiring a full-time coordinator.

For individuals such as the woman engaged in the development of the clothes closet, the linkage teams seem to create continuous learning opportunities, promote inquiry and dialogue, and encourage collaboration and team learning—all characteristics of learning organizations, according to Watkins and Marsick (1999). Like learning organizations, the linkage team becomes a system to capture and share the learning, inspire members toward a collective vision, connect them to the community, and provide leadership for learning.

Conclusion

Clearly, the investigation into learning raised more questions than it answered about the role of learning in collaboration. Learning should be added as one of the essential elements in developing interagency collaboration at the local level. The nature of this learning needs to be explored further, including how it connects to learning theory and how the group as an entity learns. Although most individuals participating in the survey characterized the learning as both individual and group, the nature of the group learning needs further examination. On the surface, it seems to have similarities with that of communities of practice and learning organizations, but does it have other dimensions? For example, is it also transformative in nature for some individuals?

It did not appear that the linkage teams were conscious of the role of learning in their collaborative efforts. They did not think of themselves as either communities of practice or learning organizations. Although learning seemed to play an important role in their success, it was not mentioned during the case studies. Helping collaborative groups become more conscious of the role of learning might be a strategy for increasing their effectiveness. How this can be done is another area for exploration.

Under the right conditions, collaborative teams, such as those formed through For the Common Good, are learning communities. Adult educators can play a role in fostering such groups by helping them become conscious of the role of learning in achieving their goals for collaboration.

References

Feden, P. D. "About Instruction: Powerful New Strategies Worth Knowing." *Educational Horizons,* Fall 1994, 73(1), 18–24.

Fulmer, R. M., and Keys, J. B. "A Conversation with Peter Senge: New Developments in Organizational Learning." *Organizational Dynamics,* Autumn 1998, 27(2), 33–42.

Imel, S. *Local Interagency Linkage Team Follow-Up Report: Ohio At-Risk Linkage Team Project.* Columbus: Center on Education and Training for Employment, The Ohio State University, 1992. (ED 347 406)

Imel, S. *For the Common Good: Local Interagency Linkage Team Second Follow-Up Report.* Columbus: Center on Education and Training for Employment, The Ohio State University, 1994. (ED 374 324)

Imel, S. *For the Common Good: Interagency Linkage Team 1997 Follow-Up Survey Results.* Unpublished report, 1997.

Imel, S., and Zengler, C. J. *For the Common Good: Local Linkage Team Case Studies.* Columbus: Center on Education and Training for Employment, The Ohio State University, 1999. (ED 435 046)

Imel, S., and Zengler, C. J. "For the Common Good: Identifying Elements of Successful Collaboration." Paper presented at the Midwest Research to Practice Conference, Madison, Wis., Sept. 27–29, 2000.

Mattessich, P. W., and Monsey, B. A. *Collaboration: What Makes It Work: A Review of the Research Literature on Factors Influencing Successful Collaboration.* St. Paul, Minn.: Amherst H. Wilder Foundation, 1992.

Merriam, S. B., and Caffarella, R. S. *Learning in Adulthood.* (2nd ed.) San Francisco: Jossey-Bass, 1999.

Schorr, L. S. *Common Purpose: Strengthening Families and Neighborhoods to Rebuild America.* New York: Anchor, 1997.

Senge, P. "Sharing Knowledge." *Executive Excellence,* June 1998, *15*(6), 11–12.

Stamps, D. "Communities of Practice: Learning Is Social, Training Is Irrelevant?" *Training,* Feb. 1997, pp. 34–42.

Watkins, K., and Marsick, V. *Sculpting the Learning Organization.* San Francisco: Jossey-Bass, 1993.

Watkins, K., and Marsick, V. "Sculpting the Learning Community: New Forms of Working and Organizing." *NASSP Bulletin,* Feb. 1999, *83*(604), 78–87.

Wenger, E. *Communities of Practice: Learning, Meaning, and Identity.* New York: Cambridge University Press, 1998.

Wenger, E., and Snyder, W. "Communities of Practice: The Organizational Frontier." *Harvard Business Review,* Jan.-Feb. 2000, pp. 139–145.

Wood, D. J., and Gray, B. "Toward a Comprehensive Theory of Evaluation." *Journal of Applied Behavioral Science,* June 1991, *27*(2), 139–167.

SUSAN IMEL, senior research specialist at the Center on Education and Training for Employment, The Ohio State University, College of Education, directs For the Common Good and the ERIC Clearinghouse on Adult, Career, and Vocational Education.

CYNTHIA J. ZENGLER is an adult basic and literacy education consultant with the Ohio Department of Education, Columbus.

4

This chapter explores some aspects of learning communities in organizations, with a special focus on manager-employee power relationships and the challenges of establishing learning organizations in traditional hierarchical organizations.

Organizational Learning Communities and the Dark Side of the Learning Organization

Phillip H. Owenby

Learning communities in organizations are nothing new. Indeed, one may argue that viable organizations are fundamentally made up of learning communities (de Geus, 1997; St. Clair, 1998). Learning communities in organizations have many forms and names—for example, learning networks (Poell, Van der Krogt, and Wildemeerch, 1999), project-based learning teams (Poell, Van der Krogt, and Warmerdam, 1998), self-directed work teams (Orsburn, Moran, Musselwhite, and Zenger, 1990), quality teams or circles (Walton, 1986), and action learning teams (Yorks, O'Neil, and Marsick, 1999). Other learning communities, such as formal or informal special interest groups of members of similar occupational or disciplinary backgrounds, are also common in organizations (Poell, Van der Krogt, and Wildemeerch, 1999). Perhaps the most discussed of all types of organizational learning communities in recent years is the learning organization (Senge, 1990a, 1990b; Watkins and Marsick, 1993). Many companies have become enamored of the learning organization concept—of turning the entire workforce into a grand learning community. Seizing on ideas that promise competitive advantage, this has fostered a headlong rush into varied initiatives such as corporate universities, knowledge management, knowledge transfer, and related practices (Jacques, 1996). For example, according to Jeanne Meister (1998), the number of corporate universities increased from about four hundred to over one thousand in the decade ending in 1998. I will argue in this chapter that learning communities in organizations—especially the so-called learning organization—are successful to

the extent that they are horizontal in nature. I will further argue that deliberate attempts to establish learning organizations must consider the mani-
fold aspects of power relations, including organizational structure, if they
are to succeed in ways that maintain the commonly held values of adult
educators.

Learning Networks as Learning Communities

There are many possible ways to describe learning communities. However,
the case could be made that any conceivable workplace learning community could be put in the framework of Poell, Van der Krogt, and
Wildemeerch's (1999) four types of learning networks.

Four Types of Learning Networks. In the *vertical learning network,*
managers and human resource development (HRD) staff direct and linearly
plan the learning activities of employees around, for example, the development and implementation of a new policy, process, goal, or procedure. The
result is a "task-specific" learning program that is "centrally organized" (p.
45). Quality circles and corporate universities easily fit this definition.

The *horizontal learning network,* in contrast, is an egalitarian, problem-
focused community of learners attempting to "solve complex problems by
reflecting on experiences, developing joint action theories, and bringing
these into practice in an investigative manner" (Poell, Van der Krogt, and
Wildemeerch, 1999, p. 45). Action learning teams and project-based learning teams easily fit the definition of this kind of network (Poell, Van der
Krogt, and Warmerdam, 1998). Such teams are defined by the way through
which they "organize [their] learning path" by diagnosing "existing conditions, developments, and problems. . . . data feedback and. . . . formulation
of learning themes; and. . . . [organizing] one or more learning projects" (p.
29). This is the ideal behind the learning organization concept.

The *external learning network,* the third kind, is "inspired by action theories developed outside the organization" (Poell, Van der Krogt, and
Wildemeerch, 1999, p. 45). It is common among professionals whose practice inside the organization is often directed by professional associations
outside the organization. For example, groups of physicians, nurses, psychologists, accountants, engineers, scientists, and others are organized
around special occupational or disciplinary interests.

Last, in the *liberal learning network,* employees direct their own learning activities, mostly in an unstructured fashion. "They may team up with
other learners for group reflection on their experiences, but basically all
individual members create their own policies and practices" (Poell, Van der
Krogt, and Wildemeerch, 1999, p. 46). Such networks would include learning communities organized around special interests, including electronic
discussion groups. As a case in point, my own organization has recently
attempted to facilitate learning communities by providing space for

electronic newsgroups—similar to USENET Internet discussion groups—on its intranet servers.

Horizontal Learning Organizations. Poell, Van der Krogt, and Warmerdam (1998) help make the case that project-based learning teams can serve as nuclei for the formation of learning organizations. As members of such learning teams develop their learning networks, the interactions among these networks "gradually become institutionalized" (p. 33) into new organizational structures that influence both learning programs and the overall learning climate. These new organizational structures, I believe, are largely horizontal. Thus, the learning organization can be understood as an interactive and interparticipatory complex of smaller learning communities or networks. In other words, it can be seen as a grand horizontal learning community.

The Dark Side of the Learning Organization

Previously identified issues that affect adult learning in general also affect the functioning of learning communities or networks, especially in the case of vertical learning networks with their top-down direction of learning goals and structures (Poell, Van der Krogt, and Wildemeerch, 1999). These issues also affect the functioning of the learning organization, particularly when channeled through institutions such as corporate universities or more traditional HRD functions.

Power Interests and the Learning Agenda. Tisdell (1993), for example, describes how subtle issues of status and power resulting from classism, racism, and sexism affect relations in learning environments by influencing participation, relationships among learners and facilitators, and ultimately what is learned both explicitly and implicitly. Similarly, Mills, Cervero, Langone, and Wilson (1995) reported how the planning of learning programs is influenced not only by available resources but also by organizational structure, culture, and power relationships. They point out that structure, culture, and power relationships operate through traditionalist interests to select which needs should be served in learning programs. Korten (1995) has pointed out how present-day corporations routinely sacrifice the interests of their employees to further corporate goals of profitability and competitive advantage in the new global economy. It could be argued that, to the extent that employee needs and interests are ignored, the corporation's attempt to deploy the collective learning power of its employees in order to obtain competitive advantage is merely a new form of worker exploitation.

Corporate Universities as Instruments of Corporate Control. In the case of corporate universities—which are in many ways admirable structures for unifying and focusing an organization's learning agendas to support its strategic business goals (Meister, 1998)—those same agendas are usually dominated by the views of executives, strategic planners, external consultants, and HRD experts. For example, a recent book entitled *Learning from the CEO: How Chief Executives Shape Corporate Education* (Meister, 2000) lists seven roles for chief executive officers in corporate learning organizations: visionary, sponsor, governor, subject matter expert, faculty, learner, and chief marketing agent. Interestingly, the role of governor is defined as taking "an active role in governing the corporate learning function, [reviewing] goals and objectives, and [providing] direction on how to measure the effectiveness of learning, and. . . . outcomes" (p. 5). Also interesting is how the role of faculty is defined as "thought leader. . . . for the entire organization" (p. 5). The book seems congratulatory of executives who champion learning, yet lacks critical awareness of their power to suppress competing agendas. And although it could be argued that most corporate universities and HRD staffs attempt to analyze learners' needs before planning and implementing learning programs, it could also be argued that the very methodologies chosen to gather and analyze learning needs are influenced by the interests of management. For example, Meister (2000) is quite clear that a primary focus of executive involvement in corporate learning is to increase "stockholder value" (p. 3). Executive-driven learning agendas can easily interfere with employee-driven learning agendas; according to recent Gallop findings employees' loyalty and retention are linked to the availability of learning and development opportunities not necessarily related to their present jobs (Buckingham and Coffman, 1999).

The Language of Power in Organizational Learning. Rees, Cervero, Moshi, and Wilson (1997) describe how organizational power interests shape the language that frames learning programs so that those interests are served rather than other, less powerful interests. Although their study focused on the way program planners exerted power through language, the implications are clear that the language employed in framing the agendas of organizational learning programs helps ensure that learning serves the dominant power interests. Indeed, the language chosen to express learning agendas works automatically and unconsciously to exclude competing agendas. In corporate learning organizations, management exercises a monopoly of language to serve the learning goals established externally to the employee-learner. This monopoly is exercised through statements of corporate mission, vision, values, strategic business objectives, and the formal learning objectives of education and training programs.

Organizational Learning as a Technology of Power. As a corporate educator and internal consultant, I have personally experienced the resistance and alienation of learners compelled to attend so-called continuous learning programs, which they had no voice in formulating and whose goals they felt were unrelated either to their daily work or their personal development goals. Far from feeling empowered in their learning (*empowerment* means allowing employees greater voice and participation in decision making about work-related issues), they felt coerced and disempowered. I would thus argue that the rhetoric of the learning organization, as in public educational institutions, constitutes a "technology of power" that is "given concrete expression in forms of knowledge that constitute the formal curriculum" (Giroux, 1990, p. 197).

Contradictions in the Quest for Organizational Learning

Toffler (1980, 1990) has stated that over recent decades organizations have begun either consciously or unconsciously to respond to the shift from the *second wave* (smokestack-industrial) to the *third wave* (postindustrial or knowledge-based) world. Jacques (1996) has argued that the rhetoric of the learning organization is in some ways an inadequate attempt to address postindustrial management challenges by repackaging systems theory in faddist language. Whatever the merits of his position, I believe that organizational learning—as a specific strategy of response to such challenges—must be accompanied by changes in the structure of power relations in organizations if it is to be faithful to its claims.

According to Toffler (1990), the traditional hierarchical model of workplace governance does not fit the requirements for success for the new kind of knowledge worker. In addition, de Geus (1997), who is widely credited with establishing the concept of the learning organization, in describing the so-called *living company* flatly declares that "centralization of power. . . . reduces the learning capacity of an organization" (p. 190). What, then, is the result when traditionally hierarchical organizations attempt to implement a learning organization culture? Based on both personal experience in consulting in organizations and the published literature, I believe that the following dynamics come into play.

Critical Awareness Versus Surplus Control. First of all, organizational learning requires not only knowledge but also critical reflection and collaborative learning skills (Cranton, 1996). These skills may often be developed among an organization's members through formal training programs or through project assignments in problem solving, quality improvement, process improvement, or action learning teams. They may even be produced as a result of deliberate changes in the leadership style of individual managers—for example, in so-called fusion leadership, which emphasizes nonhierarchical, egalitarian approaches to organizational management (Daft and Lengel, 1998). Through such programs, employees develop knowledge- and perspective-sharing networks outside the organization's normal, hierarchical silos. However, once they have been acquired, these skills and networks can be directed at all facets of the organization, including how power and privilege benefit some members rather than others at the expense of total organizational efficacy. Such insights frequently come after instances when management tacitly punishes employees for attempting to apply in unforeseen ways the principles and techniques they learned in sanctioned learning programs. For example, an employee process improvement team will uncover cause-and-effect relationships affecting their performance that originate in management practices. Often, these same management practices originate in organizational mechanisms that manifest themselves in overly centralized controls (de Geus, 1997), leading to *surplus order,* which Toffler (1990) defines as the amount of power used to establish order "over and above that needed. . . . to function. . . . [and which is] imposed merely to perpetuate the regime" (p. 470) . Thus, surplus order can be viewed as surplus control or surplus power. Toffler believes that power exercised in this way is immoral. More important, employees themselves view surplus order as immoral and tend to become cynical and less productive the more they become aware of it.

Toffler's views are reinforced by philosopher John Rawls's (1971) theory of justice. It justifies exercising power and privilege only to the extent that they benefit the total membership of the society or organization. It is in often those very areas of surplus power in which opportunities for improvement are identified by critical reflection and learning. This is because surplus power consumes or redirects energy and resources away from other functions; therefore, it is an indirect tax on organizational productivity. For example, micromanagement is a classic exercise of surplus power through which management seeks to control all the actions of subordinates, preapprove all but the most trivial decisions, and control all information flow through hierarchical channels. Micromanagement can occur when managers jealously protect mechanisms of surplus control. It is almost always evident that there is micromanagement if work flow slows or stops when the manager is absent from the office. Interestingly, micromanagement has been identified as one of the top reasons why employees leave supervisors to seek jobs elsewhere (Buckingham and Coffman, 1999).

Organizational Learning Versus Organizational Lacunae. Because those who exercise surplus control are threatened by critical awareness, they are motivated (both overtly and covertly) to defend areas of organizational practice that are threatened by agents of organizational learning, such as workers, adult educators, trainers, or organizational development consultants. These agents may be unaware but sincere organizational citizens who reveal contradictions innocently or aware corporate "revolutionaries" who reveal contradictions deliberately and knowingly. Management may protect the status quo by suppressing or redirecting learning or inquiry, or suppressing or redirecting agents of organizational learning. Suppression can result in organizational *lacunae* or blind spots (Goleman, 1985). Lacunae are areas unavailable to observation and analysis as a result of shared complacency, disguise, or misdirection. Like the air we breathe, they are largely unnoticed. Further, the fact that they are unnoticed is also unnoticed. We do not know what we do not know. These lacunae operate to obstruct the implementation of the learning organization by sapping energy and resources through surplus control or by hiding opportunities for transformation. Employees may sabotage their own consciousness to avoid punishment. Organizational cynicism can increase through awareness of how power interests serve themselves and suppress learning. These lacunae also affect the organization overtly in the form of "busy work" teams or impressive-sounding but impotent or irrelevant initiatives (in terms of fundamental or heartfelt issues). For example, employees may be assigned to process improvement teams whose charters carefully restrict the issues available for inquiry; on the off-chance that team members find legitimate ways to go beyond the charter's intended limits, budgetary or other plausible reasons can usually be found for suppressing their recommendations.

Self-Deceptive Learning Organizations. Yet relatively trivial issues can yield returns when subjected to reflection and learning. Thus, organizations may deceive themselves into believing they are successful learning organizations. Power interests may even consent to overt changes in the formal organization, especially if they can help them gain advantage over competing interests. Corporate universities in particular can deceive themselves into believing that they are agents of fundamental change when in fact they are often allowed to function only to the degree that they may be co-opted by the deep structure of power relations in the organization.

Overcoming the Dark Side

But it need not be this way. Employees, management, and other stakeholders all benefit from the success of learning organizations. Employees want the organization to succeed so that their jobs are protected, they gain satisfaction from their work, and they achieve personal developmental goals. Management wants security, continued influence over the direction of the organization, and the approval of stockholders and stakeholders. Stockholders and other stakeholders want to benefit from the success of management and employees in making the organization productive, profitable, and socially responsible. How can these interests be reconciled and served by the learning organization? The transition to the learning organization involves some growing pains.

Create a Vision. As a classic second-wave smokestack industry (Toffler, 1980), a large Southeastern company has been driven by many of the *powershift* issues identified by Toffler in 1990 to adapt to a third wave (knowledge industry) world. Since 1994, this company has undertaken initiatives designed to improve its social, environmental, and financial performance—changes that benefit its stakeholders and customers. Through its corporate university, it has also made available more continuous learning opportunities for its employees in information technology, critical problem solving skills, business awareness, environmental responsibility, leadership, teamwork, and individual development. Yet these initiatives, although laudable, did not address the issues of misused power and surplus control.

Champion New Values. In 1997, the company launched a fundamental transformation initiative to align individual and organizational behavior to its stated corporate values. This was a multifaceted initiative. First, every employee from the board of directors to the boilermakers attended a two-day workshop on interpersonal relations, communication, and other related topics; these were discussed in the context of basic values. Next an intensive awareness campaign was launched to highlight the values along with the message that it was not just OK but mandatory to hold everyone accountable for demonstrating the values in everyday work life. After that, a second phase of workshops was launched to target organizational leaders. These were accompanied by the message that leaders would be held accountable in their performance reviews for how they practice a set of "winning behaviors." Interestingly, these winning behaviors are directed toward the proper uses of power in leader-follower relationships. In tandem with this second phase of workshops, an "organizational health index" was developed using metrics derived from employee perception surveys in specific organizations. These are a kind of report card that compare organizations against statistically derived indices; scores below the control limits are colored red whereas those above are green. Managers who fail to improve the poor scores of their organizations fall under scrutiny and could risk losing their performance bonuses. A third phase of workshops is now being planned for other employees as well.

Do Not Miss the Point. This example demonstrates that a comprehensive effort to change the culture of power, when combined with a business plan that acknowledges the organization's responsibilities to all stakeholders as well as a continuous learning system for all employees, can create many—but not all—of the fundamental requisites for a healthy learning organization. To be sure, this company has attempted to graft these initiatives onto a top-down, hierarchical, second-wave organization that is little changed in management structure from the early decades of the twentieth century. As a result, some interesting dynamics have been illuminated; the traditional manner in which power is structured and distributed interferes with the espoused values of the organization. Such structural contradictions are apparent when managers are punished for actions that conflict with the corporate values but also for failing to follow management practices of the traditionally vertical organizational hierarchy. This is the implicit contradiction that comes from placing horizontal values in a stubbornly vertical organizational framework.

Conclusion

Organizations that are thoroughly committed to transformational learning must provide the widest possible training in critical reflection and action inquiry to ensure the widest possible transformational consciousness among their members. They must commit to uncovering hidden power relationships and eliminating surplus control. They must struggle to correlate the formal organization with centers of power that promote rather than obstruct organizational learning. Finally, they must realize that the formal organization needs to parallel the fundamentally horizontal structure of the learning organization. In addition to their formal roles, corporate educators, trainers, and consultants are challenged to promote the political consciousness required for a healthy learning organization.

References

Buckingham, M., and Coffman, C. *First Break All the Rules: What the World's Greatest Managers Do Differently.* New York: Simon & Schuster, 1999.

Cranton, P. "Types of Group Learning." In S. Imel (ed.), *Learning Groups: Exploring Fundamental Principles, New Uses, and Emerging Opportunities.* New Directions for Adult and Continuing Education, no. 71. San Francisco: Jossey-Bass, 1996.

Daft, R. L., and Lengel, R. H. *Fusion Leadership: Unlocking the Subtle Forces That Change People and Organizations.* San Francisco: Berrett-Koehler, 1998.

de Geus, A. *The Living Company: Habits for Survival in a Turbulent Business Environment.* Boston: Harvard Business School Press, 1997.

Giroux, H. A. "Critical Theory and the Politics of Culture and Voice: Rethinking the Discourse of Educational Research." In R. R. Sherman and R. B. Webb (eds.), *Qualitative Research in Education: Focus and Methods.* London: Falmer Press, 1990. (Originally published 1988.)

Goleman, D. *Vital Lies, Simple Truths: The Psychology of Self-Deception.* New York: Simon & Schuster, 1985.

Jacques, R. *Manufacturing the Employee: Management Knowledge from the 19th to 21st Centuries.* London: Sage, 1996.

Korten, D. C. *When Corporations Rule the World.* West Hartford, Conn.: Kumarian Press–San Francisco: Berrett-Koehler, 1995.

Meister, J. C. *Corporate Universities: Lessons in Building a World-Class Workforce.* New York: McGraw-Hill, 1998.

Meister, J. C. *Learning from the CEO: How Chief Executives Shape Corporate Education.* New York: Corporate University Exchange–Forbes Custom Publishing, 2000.

Mills, D. P., Cervero, R. M., Langone, C. A., and Wilson, A. "The Impact of Interests, Power Relationships, and Organizational Structure on Program Planning Practice: A Case Study." *Adult Education Quarterly,* 1995, *46*(1), 1–16.

Orsburn, J. D., Moran, L., Musselwhite, E., and Zenger, J. H. *Self-Directed Work Teams: The New American Challenge.* Homewood, Ill.: Irwin, 1990.

Poell, R. F., Van der Krogt, F. J., and Warmerdam, J.H.M. "Project-Based Learning in Professional Organizations." *Adult Education Quarterly,* 1998, *49*(1), 28–42.

Poell, R. F., Van der Krogt, F. J., and Wildemeerch, D. "Strategies in Organizing Work-Related Learning Projects." *Human Resource Development Quarterly,* 1999, *10*(1), 43–62.

Rawls, J. *A Theory of Justice.* Boston: Harvard University Press, 1971.

Rees, E. F., Cervero, R. M., Moshi, L., and Wilson, A. L. "Language, Power, and Construction of Adult Education Programs." *Adult Education Quarterly,* 1997, *46*(2), 63–77.

Senge, P. M. *The Fifth Discipline: The Art and Practice of the Learning Organization.* New York: Doubleday, 1990a.

Senge, P. M. "The Leader's New Work: Building Learning Organizations." *Sloan Management Review,* 1990b, *32*(1), 7–23.
St. Clair, R. "On the Commonplace: Reclaiming Community in Adult Education." *Adult Education Quarterly,* 1998, *49*(1), 5–14.
Tisdell, E. J. "Interlocking Systems of Power, Privilege, and Oppression in Adult Higher Education Classes." *Adult Education Quarterly,* 1993, *43*(4), 203–226.
Toffler, A. *The Third Wave.* New York: Bantam, 1980.
Toffler, A. *Powershift: Knowledge, Wealth, and Violence at the Edge of the 21st Century.* New York: Bantam, 1990.
Walton, M. *The Deming Management Method.* New York: Perigee-Putnam, 1986.
Watkins, K. E., and Marsick, V. J. *Sculpting the Learning Organization: Lessons in the Art and Science of Systemic Change.* San Francisco: Jossey-Bass, 1993.
Yorks, L., O'Neil, J., and Marsick, V. J. (eds.). *Action Learning: Successful Strategies for Individual, Team, and Organizational Development.* Advances in Developing Human Resources, no. 2. San Francisco: Berrett-Koehler, 1999.

PHILLIP H. OWENBY is a senior learning consultant, curricula manager, and faculty member for a corporate university. He also teaches graduate courses in adult learning and organizational management at Tusculum College in Knoxville, Tennessee.

5

The extent to which practitioner inquiry groups function as democratic learning communities depends largely on how a facilitator negotiates the group's power relationships and politics.

Negotiating Power and Politics in Practitioner Inquiry Communities

Cassandra Drennon

For nearly a decade, the field of adult literacy education has been exploring the potential of practitioner inquiry staff development, a form of teacher research, for producing knowledge and improving service to learners. Practitioner inquiry groups are organized as learning communities. Group members, who generally are classroom teachers and program administrators, come together over time to collaborate on practice-based problems. The idea is for practitioners to reflect critically together on their practice, engage in meaningful dialogue with one another, conduct systematic inquiries into practice, and in some cases even take collective action that will effect change in classrooms, programs, or policies (Altrichter, Posch, and Somekh, 1993; Carr and Kemmis, 1986; Kemmis, 1993; Lytle, Belzer, and Reumann, 1992). At the core of the practitioner inquiry movement are democratic beliefs that teachers, program administrators, and other practitioners should have a significant voice in determining how the work of literacy education is carried out. Moreover, they have an ethical role to play in efforts toward a more just society.

As a facilitator, I have often felt discontinuity between my democratic aims and the reality of inquiry groups. For example:

- I want these learning communities to be inclusive of all members, yet it is not a given that people will be respected for who they are and what they believe simply because they have a common purpose.
- Although I may be able to encourage conversations that are "reflective," it is much more difficult to promote dialogue that is "critical."

NEW DIRECTIONS FOR ADULT AND CONTINUING EDUCATION, no. 95, Fall 2002 © Wiley Periodicals, Inc.

- Although I try to promote collaboration and collegiality, group members may prefer to pursue their learning individually.
- Although I want inquiry communities to be places where participants can pursue the questions about practice that intrigue them most, it is often apparent that teachers' supervisors are establishing from the sidelines questions that can and cannot be pursued.
- There is often tension between a group's desire for a high level of direction from me, and my desire for the group to claim its own authority.

In essence, my experiences have not always matched the images of inquiry groups that originally inspired me, such as this one offered by Lytle (1996):

> All involved seem to be seeking to alter aspects of the existing structures and power relationships. . . . In forming and building the inquiry community, participants took a critical stance. They questioned common practice, deliberated about what they regarded as expert knowledge, examined underlying assumptions, and attempted to unpack the arrangements and structures of adult literacy education to understand their sources and impacts. In addition, each of their individual projects had the potential to stimulate some form of change, first through its implementation and dissemination on site and second through the seminar as a collaborative community. The participants' collective work suggests that these kinds of practitioner inquiry communities regard educational problems and issues not solely as individual matters but also as social, cultural, and political concerns that may require collective action. [pp. 92–93]

Vivid depictions such as this were the inspiration behind many recent efforts to organize learning communities for practitioner inquiry in the United States. However, they were not able to make the effort any easier because they are constructed as if the material realities of the world are not being played out. In many respects, these accounts *suggest* an evenness of habit and mind, a homogeneity, and a balance of power not typically reflected in groups. Moreover, the facilitator is invisible; critical reflection, dialogue, and action just seem to happen. In a more realistic depiction, facilitators would be central in the effort to democratize knowledge production in inquiry groups, yet they would struggle to do so in the cross-currents of internally and externally based power dynamics.

It was out of my own struggles as a facilitator enacting democratic practice and my desire to understand those struggles better that I set out to talk with other inquiry group facilitators about their experiences. The remainder of this chapter draws not only on the literature but also on interviews with women who facilitate adult literacy practitioner inquiry communities in the United States (Drennon, 2000). It focuses on the intersection of practice, ethical aims, and power relationships to explain why practitioner inquiry communities are never the wholly democratic learning communities we wish them to be. The point in demystifying practitioner inquiry communities is not to discredit the inquiry movement. On the contrary, by understanding how it is that the usual practices we engage in as facilitators become sites of struggle, choices reveal themselves to us. Practitioner inquiry groups, like other learning communities, will never wholly achieve our democratic ideals, but they *can* be more democratic. Naming the challenges that facilitators encounter in the struggle for democracy is an essential step toward negotiating the possibilities of these learning communities with greater acumen.

Power and Politics in Practitioner Inquiry Groups

Facilitation of practitioner inquiry groups involves at least three broad categories of practice. First, facilitators are central in developing and sustaining the group as a learning community. Toward this end, they might recruit group members, see to it that meeting agendas are planned and carried out, and promote an ethos of collaboration, collegiality, and shared purpose in the group. Second, facilitators take the lead in facilitating learning in the group. They help participants raise practice-based concerns, structure opportunities for critical reflection and dialogue, assist participants in the framing of research questions, and support group members as they collect, analyze, and report on data. Third, facilitators of inquiry groups are almost always involved in the effort to advance the status of inquiry and practitioner knowledge in programs and the profession. Thus, they might guide group members through the process of writing up research for publication or help them plan and organize presentations for conferences or other staff development events.

Facilitators can experience virtually any day-to-day practice as a site of struggle—that is, a moment in time when the group's democratic impulse is somehow thwarted. A key reason why day-to-day practices become sites of struggle is that power relationships and politics play out inside as well as outside the boundaries of inquiry groups.

Power and Politics Inside the Group. To say that asymmetrical relations of power are pervasive in inquiry groups is to say that individuals are always ranked in relation to one another—as they are in the larger society—hierarchically. In a hierarchy based on socially structured power, relationships are based on characteristics that individuals are generally born with or born into. These include race, class, gender, sexuality, regionality, able-bodiedness, and other identity categories. A hierarchy of organizationally structured power relationships is also present in inquiry groups. In this sense, relationships are based on role status. For example, because the facilitator is the group leader, there is an asymmetrical power relationship between her and the rest of the group. There is also unequal power inherent in the relationship between teachers and program administrators who may work together as members of the same inquiry group, or between full-time teachers and those who only work part-time. The category of organizationally structured power also refers to the status of an inquiry group in a larger educational system. Actually, hierarchies are not exclusive of one another. Those people granted the most privilege in society by virtue of race, class, and gender, for instance, have often been the same ones to achieve greater organizational status. Arguably, knowledge and skill are socially distributed as well. Moreover, the personality traits, habits, and attitudes that privilege some members of an inquiry group, place some at a disadvantage, and render others a liability generally reflect dominant cultural values and norms that have continually been legitimated by society or institutions.

Power and Politics Outside the Group. An educational system can support practitioner inquiry as individual professional development and yet actually challenge the democratic aims of inquiry by being at odds with its critical perspective and orientation toward change. Foucault (1980) defined *regime of truth* as "the types of discourse that society accepts and makes function as true" (p. 131). A regime of truth operates in educational organizations through regulatory and stabilizing functions. Popkewitz (1987) explains, "They shape and fashion what can be said and what must be left unsaid, the types of discourse accepted as true and the mechanisms that make it possible to distinguish between truth and error" (pp. 4–5). It is not surprising that many organizations will not support practitioners' critical examination of their own policies. Group members who have internalized the regime of truth support the organization's power by opting for "safe" inquiry projects that will not disrupt the status quo.

Organizations' structures can also constrain a group's democratic agenda from the outside. Organizations may limit the time that practitioners are able to engage with classroom research or with colleagues in a group setting. They can also limit or deny the structured opportunities for practitioners to extend their knowledge to wider audiences. The pressure to produce reports, which can readily shift a group's emphasis from process to end product, is another mechanism through which educational systems constrain a group's democratic impulse.

Democratic staff development has little chance of thriving unless larger educational institutions express a commitment to democratic culture (Gore, 1998; Gore and Zeichner, 1995; Kemmis, 1993; Noffke, 1992, 1997). Facilitators, however, can get mixed messages from the larger educational organizations that ostensibly support inquiry. Moreover, they may see themselves as generally unable to effect changes on the organizational level when they are very much a part of, and dependent on, the "system" that practitioner inquiry potentially seeks to alter. Although organizations may provide funding, they are often structured in ways that work against the level of engagement that practitioner inquiry requires. Despite a facilitator's commitment to democratic principles of practitioner inquiry, she may feel obligated to negotiate the competing and sometimes contradictory interests of the state—her employer.

Negotiating Power Issues and Politics

There are at least three significant power issues that facilitators encounter in practitioner inquiry communities. First, they often struggle with their own identity as it is either socially or organizationally constructed. When this happens the questions become these: What does it mean to be an authority in a democratic culture? Or what does it mean to be white or African American or young or a lesbian in this group? Second, facilitators struggle with the identity of the group itself. The question becomes: What does it mean for this group to be an inquiry group and not something else? Third, facilitators struggle with the identity of practitioner inquiry as a movement. This leads to such questions as these: What does it mean to advance practitioners' knowledge in the larger field? And what kind of knowledge and whose knowledge is it that we advance or not, and for what reasons? The questions arise because of competing interests brought to bear on democratic aims in a given scenario. To resolve the questions, the facilitator needs to exercise power through the negotiation of her own and others' interests.

An analytical framework developed by Cervero and Wilson (1994, 1998) offers a way to understand how social and organizational power relationships operate through day-to-day practices in practitioner inquiry communities. Cervero and Wilson assert that educators negotiate *with* and *among* personal, social, and organizational interests to achieve their practical purposes and the democratic aims associated with them. In this sense, facilitating practitioner inquiry is always a political process. They conceive of negotiation as the central mechanism of power because of the term's political connotation. Negotiation, they explain, is "a process by which people confer, discuss, and bargain in order to reach agreement about what to do in relation to the educational program" (p. 6). Their framework also takes into account negotiation at a more fundamental level where educators negotiate simultaneously *about* interests and power relationships of stakeholders.

In practitioner inquiry, there is a surface level of negotiation where facilitators go about getting things done in a practical sense while guided by democratic aims. Cervero and Wilson refer to negotiations on this surface level as *substantive negotiations* because they are about the substance of the practitioner inquiry program—the activities, the methods, and the practical outcomes that are desired. In substantive negotiations, facilitators act *within* the web of power relationships. There is also a process of negotiation occurring simultaneously on a deeper level *about* issues of power. These issues are fundamentally about social and organizational identity, the group identity, or the public identity of practitioner inquiry. Cervero and Wilson refer to negotiations occurring simultaneously on this deeper level as *metanegotiations*. It is on this level that facilitators *act on* power relations themselves, either changing them or reinforcing them. Metanegotiations, according to Cervero and Wilson, directly influence substantive negotiations. Applying this framework to the struggle facilitators experience brings some clarity to what is easily obscured through the chaos and noise of everyday practice. When facilitators negotiate among competing interests to achieve their practical and democratic aims, they are, at the same time, negotiating about competing interests and about power relationships. Through this negotiation, power relationships are effectively reproduced or transformed. Another way of explaining situations is to say that the way a facilitator negotiates the power issues she encounters in practitioner inquiry has a direct bearing on the achievement of her practical and democratic aims.

The Politics of Being Known: Negotiating Social and Organizational Identity. A facilitator's capacity to act is constructed *within* situations and *through* group relationships. She has no single identity and does not speak in a single voice. Maher and Tetreault (1996) discuss identity politics as a negotiation among "dominated and exploited groups trying to understand who they are." This involves a "struggle against the barriers between them and other groups that these same identities create" (p. 156).

Rocco and West (1998) use the term *polyrhythmic realities* to refer to "how a person can be privileged by one characteristic and at the same time not be privileged by virtue of another" (p. 173). It goes without saying that facilitators occupy a privileged position in the hierarchy of organizationally structured power relations; they are the leaders. However, in spite of leadership status, facilitators may, in relation to others, be lower-rung occupants in the social hierarchy based on identity characteristics including race, class, sexuality, geographical identity, physical attributes, or age.

Feminist poststructural theories highlight this idea of "constantly shifting identity" (Tisdell, 1998) and posit that the connection between one's identity and social structures affects positionality in learning environments. Positionality, essentially, was what an African American facilitator was referring to when she said about facilitating groups, "Your gender and your color and your social status matter. They matter big-time." The concept refers to the idea that a group member is marginal only in relation to another. Poststructural theorists argue that the capacity for agency can be enhanced if teachers and learners explore the intersection of identity and social structure rather than ignore it, because this intersection shapes the construction of knowledge (Maher and Tetreault, 1997). A lesbian facilitator with whom I spoke explained precisely how this occurs:

> So, if I'm working with lesbians and there seems to be some feminist consciousness then I assume that we have a shared body of reading, a shared

background, a shared way of deconstructing power structures or thinking about literary allusions or whatever in our work. When that's not there, you're not sure whether to count on it or not. I'd like to say that I bring [a lesbian feminist perspective into the group] but I don't know if I could really come up with ten examples. I mean, I think I might allude to it or try to bring in a quote or make some reference but it's. . . . I'm more conscious that this is not going to ring any familiar bells. This is going to be something that might feel a little unfamiliar to people or like a stretch or something like that. . . . I just use. . . . a more generic teaching-learning, sort of the things that carry currency in the field around learner-centered practice that I assume here [in this city] that people have some working knowledge of.

This facilitator is explaining how her power is contextual as well as relational. Using "generic" strategies that fail to acknowledge difference shapes the construction of knowledge in the group. She chooses to maintain the status quo or the illusion that people are all the same even though, in principle, she supports the democratic principle of engaging diverse perspectives. Similarly, an African American facilitator described how she is comfortable engaging a group in social critique based on race when she is working with other African Americans. But when working with white teachers she is not sure how she will be perceived with regard to race issues and therefore does not address them. Clinchy (1996) has said, "Both separate and connected knowing achieve their full power when practiced in partnership with other like-minded knowers" (p. 233). When facilitators feel they are working with like-minded individuals they are more inclined to engage them in critical examination of the social, cultural, and political context of literacy and learning. But this raises concerns about what happens in groups where learners are socially different.

Power dynamics in a group are constructed out of race, class, gender, regionality, and other identity categories. One facilitator, for instance, described wanting to "protect" a group member who was significantly younger than the rest of the group and then "bombing" at an activity. She acted on the situation by intervening more assertively than she might have if the struggling participant were older. "The youngness added to my sense of her vulnerability," she explained. In another group, class-based differences between one participant and the rest left the facilitator feeling that the minority group member was not "right" for practitioner inquiry. Again the concept of positionality offers a way of viewing the relational significance of identity. Tisdell (1998) notes that positionality has remained relatively unexamined in adult education literature, and this discussion supports the call for further investigation into the topic.

The Politics of Creating Knowledge: Negotiating Group Identity. Facilitators continually negotiate with group members and other stakeholders an understanding of what inquiry groups are about. Practitioner inquiry is a relatively new idea in adult literacy education.

Because the groups are in an unfamiliar situation, the process of negotiating a working consensus of what is to go on is perhaps more visible than it might be in other social arenas that practitioners function in, such as training sessions or staff meetings. Sociologists explain why this is so. "The negotiation process becomes apparent in situations that are less familiar and routine. On those occasions people are likely to be more aware of the potential gap between the private and projected definitions of various participants" (O'Brien and Kollock, 1997, p. 67).

Facilitators locate many of their struggles in participants' resistance to accepting the new norms and culture of the inquiry group. It may be that facilitators are especially concerned with maintaining the boundaries and their definition of an inquiry group because of the pressures that serve to undermine them. That is, the norms they struggle to foster are contrary to the norms that many teachers are socialized into. This is a theme that has been explored by a number of researchers interested in how the culture and norms of schooling, particularly those associated with teacher privacy and autonomy, work against the aims of teacher research (Cochran-Smith and Lytle, 1992; Holly, 1987; Little, 1990). It goes without saying that educational organizations are better established as social-cultural systems than inquiry groups. Facilitators play a central role in defining and sustaining the alternative system and this may explain, in part, the pressure they exert when it comes to encouraging the group to go about its business in very particular ways. Gore and Zeichner (1995), who have examined the strategies through which power is wielded in education, suggest that this boundary work is itself a form of power that has the effect of "integrating or normalizing all [practitioners] into a rather singular notion of what counts" (p. 208). They urge educators to be aware of the normalizing effects of boundary work.

The Politics of Being Knowers: Negotiating the Public Identity of Practitioner Inquiry.   Power issues in this category speak to different but related questions. Who is really listening to what practitioner researchers have to say? From the perspective of facilitators, what do we want them to hear? What does the wider public expect to hear from us, and what are the implications of this expectation? These questions force facilitators to wonder also about their role in shaping the content and quality of written research reports. Facilitators are dismayed when there seems to be no real audience for written reports or public presentations about field-generated research. Facilitators are motivated by how they think organizations will react to the process and outcomes of practitioner inquiry because they rely on them for continued funding. Negotiating the public identity of practitioner inquiry is in this sense closely tied to the issue of negotiating the group identity, because what goes on in the group is ultimately conveyed to outsiders. Cochran-Smith and Lytle (1998) suggest power issues associated with the public identity of practitioner inquiry when they write: "The growth of the teacher research movement hinges on a paradox: as it is used in the service of more and more agendas and even institutionalized in certain contexts, it is in danger of becoming anything and everything. As we know, however, anything and everything often lead in the end to nothing of consequence or power. It would be unfortunate indeed if the generative nature of teacher research contributed to either its marginalization and trivialization, on the one hand, or its subtle co-optation or colonization, on the other" (p. 21).

Facilitators want to ward off the threat of trivialization as well as co-optation, and this is why maintaining the boundaries and definition of the group on the one hand becomes just as important as extending the group's knowledge to wider audiences on the other. "The point," write Cochran-Smith and Lytle (1998), "is not to determine whether teacher research 'counts' but what it counts for, not whether it is 'interesting,' but whose interests it serves" (p. 33). Facilitators' stories of struggle in negotiating the public identity of practitioner inquiry shed light on the ways that real facilitators in real settings are attempting to answer this question and reconciling that effort with a democratic vision.

Rather than viewing their struggles as chaos and competing interests as just "noise," facilitators may benefit from recognizing that recurring patterns in their experience are rooted in socially and organizationally structured power relationships. Moreover, facilitators may be empowered through an understanding of their actions as political strategies and tactics that have a bearing, one way or another, on power relationships as well as democratic aims.

Conclusion

It is important that we emphasize the strategic contribution of facilitators—their strategies and tactics, as well as the consequences of their efforts—for democratic education. The fact that democracy is packed with *inherent* tensions and outright contradictions cannot be overemphasized. There is a contradiction, for instance, in the desire both to lead the group and yet to take the focus away from oneself as leader. There is an ongoing tension between the authority practitioners are given to chart the course of their own inquiry and the authority facilitators are given to stimulate a practitioner's further development and change. Facilitators cope with a persistent tension between serving the needs of the inquiry group and responding to the demands of host organizations and funding agencies. Negotiating the tensions and contradictions inherent in democratic education will always be part and parcel of the effort to enact democratic ideals in practitioner inquiry communities. These ideals can never be completely achieved, but they *can* be furthered. Practitioner inquiry facilitators can choose practices that are more democratic than others and they can continually examine the direction and effects of routine practices, power issues, and the political responses to power that different actors employ. Given the contradictions and ironies inherent in democratic practice, facilitators can develop their own healthy skepticism about the aims they seek to achieve and interrogate all practices for their effect on individuals and groups.

References

Altrichter, H., Posch, P., and Somekh, B. *Teachers Investigate Their Work: An Introduction to the Methods of Action Research.* New York: Routledge, 1993.

Carr, W., and Kemmis, S. *Becoming Critical: Education, Knowledge, and Action Research.* Bristol, Pa.: Falmer Press, 1986.

Cervero, R. M., and Wilson, A. L. *Planning Responsibly for Adult Education: A Guide to Negotiating Power and Interests.* San Francisco: Jossey-Bass, 1994.

Cervero, R. M., and Wilson, A. L. "Working the Planning Table: The Political Practice of Adult Education." *Studies in Continuing Education,* 1998, *20,* 5–21.

Clinchy, B. M. "Connected and Separate Knowing: Toward a Marriage of Two Minds." In N. Goldberger, J. Tarule, B. Clinchy, and M. Belenky (eds.), *Knowledge, Difference, and Power: Essays Inspired by Women's Ways of Knowing.* New York: Basic Books, 1996.

Cochran-Smith, M., and Lytle, S. L. "Interrogating Cultural Diversity: Inquiry and Action." *Journal of Teacher Education,* 1992, *43*(2), 104–115.

Cochran-Smith, M., and Lytle, S. L. "Teacher Research: The Question That Persists." *Leadership in Education,* 1998, *1*(1), 19–36.

Drennon, C. E. "Enacting Democratic Aims of Practitioner Inquiry in the Context of Power and Politics." Unpublished doctoral dissertation. Department of Adult Education, University of Georgia, 2000.

Foucault, M. *Power/Knowledge: Selected Interviews and Other Writings, 1972–1977.* New York: Pantheon, 1980.

Gore, J. M. "Disciplining Bodies: On the Continuity of Power Relations in Pedagogy." In T. S. Popkewitz and M. Brennan (eds.), *Foucault's Challenge: Discourse, Knowledge, and Power in Education.* New York: Teachers College Press, 1998.

Gore, J. M., and Zeichner, K. M. "Connecting Action Research to Genuine Teacher Development." In J. Smyth (ed.), *Critical Discourses on Teacher Development.* New York: Cassell, 1995.

Holly, P. "Action Research: Cul-de-Sac or Turnpike?" *Peabody Journal of Education,* 1987, *64,* 71–100.

Kemmis, S. "Action Research and Social Movement: A Challenge for Policy Research." *Educational Policy Analysis Archives,* 1993, *1*(1). [http://olam.ed.asu.edu/epaa/ v1n1.html].

Little, J. "The Persistence of Privacy: Autonomy and Initiative in Teachers' Professional Relations." *Teachers College Record,* 1990, *91,* 509–535.

Lytle, S. L. "A Wonderfully Terrible Place to Be: Learning in Practitioner Inquiry Communities." In P. Sissel (ed.), *A Community-Based Approach to Literacy Programs* (Vol. 70, pp. 85–96). San Francisco: Jossey-Bass, 1996.

Lytle, S. L., Belzer, A., and Reumann, R. "Invitations to Inquiry: Rethinking Staff Development in Adult Literacy Education." (Technical Report TR92–2). Philadelphia: University of Pennsylvania, National Center on Adult Literacy, 1992.

Maher, F. A., and Tetreault, M.K.T. "Women's Ways of Knowing in Women's Studies, Feminist Pedagogies, and Feminist Theory." In N. Goldberger, J. Tarule, B. Clinchy, and M. Belenky (eds.), *Knowledge, Difference, and Power: Essays Inspired by Women's Ways of Knowing.* New York: Basic Books, 1996.

Maher, F. A., and Tetreault, M.K.T. "Learning in the Dark: How Assumptions of Whiteness Shape Classroom Knowledge." *Harvard Educational Review*, 1997, *67*, 321–349.

Noffke, S. "The Work and Workplace of Teachers in Action Research." *Teaching and Teacher Education*, 1992, *8*(1), 15–29.

Noffke, S. "Professional, Personal, and Political Dimensions of Action Research." *Review of Research in Education*, 1997, *22*, 305–343.

O'Brien, J., and Kollock, P. (eds.). *The Production of Reality: Essays and Readings on Social Interaction* (2nd ed.). Newbury Park, Calif.: Pine Forge Press, 1997.

Popkewitz, T. S. "Ideology and Social Formation in Teacher Education." In T. S. Popkewitz (ed.), *Critical Studies in Teacher Education.* Bristol, Pa.: Falmer Press, 1987.

Rocco, T., and West, G. W. "Deconstructing Privilege: An Examination of Privilege in Adult Education." *Adult Education Quarterly*, 1998, *48*, 171–184.

Tisdell, E. J. "Poststructural Feminist Pedagogies: The Possibilities and Limitations of Feminist Emancipatory Adult Learning Theory and Practice." *Adult Education Quarterly*, 1998, *48*, 139–156.

CASSANDRA DRENNON is an educational researcher and consultant in Athens, Georgia.

6

The formation of learning communities in remote retreat settings, specifically Yukon Island in Alaska, is the focus of this chapter. Testimony by learners and facilitators is included to enhance the discussion of the learning environment, the creation of community, and the learning process.

Learning Communities in Remote Retreat Settings

Gretchen T. Bersch, Carole L. Lund

Jerold Apps (1991) writes that any comprehensive theory of adult learning must take into account three aspects: the learner, the learning process, and the context. In examining the formation of learning communities, these three aspects are pivotal. In this chapter, we will use one location—Yukon Island in Alaska—as an example of a remote retreat setting, and will explore the environment as the context for learning and building community.

Yukon Island

Yukon Island is 225 miles south of Anchorage on the tip of the Kenai Peninsula. It is the largest island in Kachemak Bay, seven miles across the water from a small town, Homer. The island has dense woods, heavy vegetation, tidal zones, and abundant sea life and wildlife, such as salmon, otters, and bald eagles. For more than three thousand years, the island has been inhabited: residents included two periods of Eskimo people; a period of Tanaina Indians, Alaska Natives influenced by Russians; and fox farmers in the early 1900s. In the 1950s Gretchen Bersch's parents homesteaded on the island with their children. From the beginning the family envisioned the island as a place for learning and education. In 2001, the island remained a remote retreat. The Yukon Island Center for Research and Education became a reality over twenty years ago. Famous scholars and students interested in adult education, marine biology, archaeology, wilderness medicine, international military exercises, writing workshops, and business have been frequent guests.

For me, the Yukon Island program was more like a learning adventure. The program gave me an opportunity to learn and experience fellowship in a place of pristine and unparalleled natural beauty. The adventure of coming to the island in a boat, passing majestic mountains and bird rookeries as we sailed on deep blue waters to the sandy shore, seemed surreal. Even the boat operators were adult educators and they gladly informed me of the history of all the beauty that mesmerized me. Never previously having a camping or outdoor living experience, on Yukon Island I was able to overcome many personal limitations. Mixing classroom learning with the natural living experience of the great outdoors was simply extraordinary. [De Bora McIntosh, personal communication with the authors, 2000]

The environment can act as a catalyst for learning and help create an exciting and productive learning experience. On Yukon Island, the natural setting, the basic comforts available, and the climate of trust all foster learning.

Natural Setting. One of the deeply held values of Alaska Native, American Indian, and First Nations peoples is respect for and appreciation of nature. Being in a beautiful place, surrounded by the sights, sounds, and smells of the woods and the sea, heightens the senses and brings one closer to nature and to oneself. On Yukon Island, participants' senses become more tuned to nature; they begin to observe and hear more sensitively. Learners step into the rhythm of life, where tides and weather and the abundance of fish and berries establish their own priorities.

When one is in a remote location there is a physical separation from all the demands of everyday life: ringing telephones, work deadlines, family chores, the pressures of everyday living. A natural setting provides a back-to-basics way of life reminiscent of pioneer days. Without the intrusion of technology, the learners on Yukon Island are able to concentrate on reflection and dialogue. They are free to focus on their learning. "Our removal from a noisy and unattractive physical environment—the average indoor classroom—greatly accelerated our learning, and gave greater meaning to the knowledge gained. I also believe we were better listeners and comprehenders of the course content (Douglas Marshall, personal communication with the authors, 2000).

Basic Comforts. Being on the island reminds us that we really do not need much in the way of creature comforts. Food, as a basic comfort, plays an important role on the island. Usually, all participants bring an item for the first evening's dinner, which is a potluck community affair. The symbolism and fact of sharing creates a feeling of communion; everyone has created dinner. All meals are taken together, family-style, usually at one long table with chairs and benches. Participants mention often that they are reminded of earlier times in their lives when they shared meals with their families. With kerosene lamps, a propane cooking stove, a large woodstove for heat, outhouses, a sauna, and no electricity or regular running water, learners experience old-fashioned, basic comforts. In *Handbook for the Soul,* Lynn Andrews writes, "As individuals and as a society, we must dig deep enough to once again touch the rich earth beneath—deep enough to find the manifestations of nature within our own souls. To do that, it is imperative to find our way into natural settings, into the wilderness. It's there that the soul is healed. It's there that we can begin to unite body and soul" (1995, p. 95).

Describing his experience on Yukon Island, one participant said: "The deep connection with the students to a large extent comes from living together in a way that includes food preparation and a joyful maintenance of the camplike setting. The teacher and students are really dependent on one another. Through their mutual tasks they have a better chance to know each other as full human beings" (Raymond Wlodkowski, personal communication with the authors, 2000).

Usually one meal is taken around the campfire; the participants cook salmon over an open fire. The ancient act of cooking over a fire, the circle formed by the group, and the breaking of bread together are full of symbolism. On this island, this act is reminiscent of the many people who have lived there before. The firepit is literally just the current one. Palmer (1998) writes, "By great things, I mean the subjects around which the circle of seekers has always gathered—not the disciplines that study these subjects, not the texts that talk about them, not the theories that explain them, but the things themselves. . . . Great things such as these are the vital nexus of community in education. It is the act of gathering around them and trying to understand them—as the first humans must have gathered around fire— that we become who we are as knowers, teachers, and learners" (p. 107). Creating an environment that evokes a simpler life, a primitive way of living, allows learners to reach inside themselves. Sharing stories around the campfire, which is part of the experience on Yukon Island, contributes to the emergence of a feeling of community.

Climate of Trust. Because of the total immersion quality of the setting, group members reach a level of trust quickly. Merely coming to the island means taking a risk for most of the learners. Learners find themselves in a rustic situation, working and living together. The communal nature of the situation and the feeling that they are surviving the elements are catalysts for them to reach deeper levels of sharing. Learners help one another feel safe. A willingness to take risks and think creatively follow.

> I was newly divorced after twenty-eight years of marriage before the Yukon Island trip and still grieving and feeling responsible for not being able to make the relationship work. While on the island my senses seemed to come alive for the first time in a long time. The familiarity of the water, salt, rain, mist, fish, tall grasses, walking on the beaches and up on the rocky cliffs was the most perfect thing for my self-nurturing and healing. The picture in my mind of our big house on Sullivan Island, the funny crazy things we did as little

kids, our inquisitiveness, fearlessness, tall tales we told each other (always
involving animals) made me smile and laugh to myself. [Barbara Fleek, personal communication with the authors, 2000]

Perhaps it is the awakening of the senses that fosters creativity. In
Creativity and Adult Education, Edelson (1999, p. 5) writes, "For adult educators the positive contribution of environment to creativity is a very significant line of thought because it can lead to an examination of educational
and work settings and how they can influence human behavior."

As the adult education literature has established, when a positive climate for learners is created it enhances their ability to learn. A natural setting and simple, basic comforts foster a climate of trust where learners are
free to take risks. Remote retreat settings that free learners from daily pressures and fears also enhance their ability to think reflectively and creatively.

Creation of Community

The community in a remote retreat setting begins to form at the moment of
arrival and continues to build throughout the session. Shifting control,
building community, and equalizing facilitator and learner roles affect the
creation of community.

Locus of Control. It is an interesting paradox that in a big city people
often feel they do not have much control over their own individual lives but
believe they do have fair control over nature. In a natural setting, the opposite is true. In dealing with the natural setting of Yukon Island, participants
soon learn that nature is in control. The locus shifts from individual to community as they work together to deal with minor discomforts. The environment is conducive to shifting from *me* to *us.*

In *Handbook for the Soul,* Phil Cousineau writes, "Perhaps this revival of
interest in the soul is reflecting a slight turn away from the isolation of indi-
vidualism back to the cohesion of community. Soulful life nudges us toward
reconnecting ourselves to the neighborhood, toward community action,
political activity, reattaching with our family, our past, our ancestors, and
revitalizing our spiritual lives. For me, it's a curious notion that soulful life
tends not to be too consumed with future or evolution; instead, soul moves
us backward, where we begin to contemplate the past" (1995, p. 162).

In every class, workshop, or retreat, some in the group are carried back
to their past, to childhood and family memories. People remember activities with their parents, and their grandparents, special times in their childhood, times of sharing and times of community. Reflection on the past
allows learners to move toward their futures.

Having been born and raised in Southeast Alaska, my weekend visit to Yukon
Island was like going home and brought back memories of my childhood.
From two to three years of age I lived on Sullivan Island (close to Haines,

Alaska) with my grandmother and grandfather. She was Tlingit and he was Norwegian. They lived a subsistence lifestyle, gillnet fishing, farming, picking wild strawberries and blueberries. That period of my life was truly enchanted. Gretchen's island started my journey not only to healing but to valuing the childhood history I'd not shared. From that time on I started talking with my three daughters about my childhood. Often we are so busy as adults with work and kids that we close ourselves off. [Barbara Fleek, personal communication with the authors, 2000]

Community Building. Building a community of learners begins for some on the way to Yukon Island as they share rides in cars and on the boat. The excitement of the adventure and the anticipation of the learning bind the group together. Cooking, eating, living, and learning together as a group for several days creates a feeling of community. The learners challenge themselves and one another to learn and understand. At times the community becomes so strong that the demarcation between learners is lost. This is not to say that all the learners think and act the same. Quite the opposite—there is a great appreciation for the diversity represented by each individual in the group. The community cares about each member; this is apparent in almost every interaction.

Although participants came to the island to achieve similar academic goals, our personal reasons for attending were probably as diverse as our characters. Even so, everyone was very positive and encouraging and truly excited about each person being there. The highly regarded adult educator who came to facilitate in the beautiful surroundings assisted us in visualizing from a worldwide perspective and aided us in developing leadership and collaborative skills. We were encouraged to utilize our full intellectual and creative capacities. The program provided a great opportunity for informal interactions between participants and the facilitator. We all felt like peers and were very comfortable socializing with an adult education professional whom we respected and admired. [De Bora McIntosh, personal communication with the authors, 2000]

Facilitator and Learner Roles. On Yukon Island, those who come to teach comment on the fact that they feel a part of the group. If the facilitators are comfortable with the space and centered in the environment, the learners will be more accepting. The facilitators provide a nurturing, safe, warm environment in which to learn. There is a natural equality of roles and dynamics between faculty and learners. The power relationship between teacher and learners almost disappears. Facilitators consciously and subconsciously work toward making everyone feel comfortable.

I learned a lot about community in that setting and it was wonderful to hear students share personal experiences in Alaska and elsewhere. It was a great group and bonding was evident. The walk on the island with the stop at the homestead house brought people to a deeper level of thought about the experience, and homemade bread and fresh salmon on the beach gave an added dimension to it all! I was particularly pleased to hear discussion of dreams as well as challenges and to learn about the way that the text and other readings stimulated reflection about community development and human development operating in tandem. [Vivian Johnson, personal communication with the authors, 2000]

Learners form their community much like the populations that inhabited Yukon Island in the past. Being in a remote retreat setting facilitates the building of a community; it enables learners and facilitators to relinquish control, fosters dependence on one another, and allows all participants to function as both learners and facilitators.

The Learning Process

The process of learning in a remote retreat setting involves the individual learner as well as the community of learners. Organic learning, collaboration, and catalysts for change influence learning during the course of the workshop and long after.

Organic Learning. Organic learning is the synthesis of the natural environment, the community of learners, and the flow of learning. The *American Heritage Dictionary* defines organic as "simple, healthful, and close to nature: an organic lifestyle; . . . constituting an integral part of a whole; fundamental" (1992, p. 1275). On Yukon Island, the beauty and music of nature provide a vivid background for learning; it counters the fatigue of everyday living. People are required to use a different set of skills; most are required to relinquish control. This loss of control contributes to the flow of learning. Barriers are broken down; there is a sharpening of the senses and a freeing of individual responsibilities and restrictions. The supportive environment and lack of attention to time contribute to learning on one's own terms.

> The retreat setting of Yukon Island was a major benefit to my education experience. There is something about being in the out-of-doors that expands my senses and my ability to learn in a more holistic manner. Nature has a kind of wisdom that teaches me to open up to possibilities, to think and feel from a place of inner knowing. I tend to blend and balance the course content with my personal meaning in a much deeper way. No longer influenced by the ticking clock, I am able to honor my own rhythm and be fully present to listen and ponder the theories and concepts introduced by the guest presenter. The discussion and dialogue often gets intense and serious. At other times, it is laced with laughter and humor. [Ann Wing Quest, personal communication with the authors, 2000]

Collaboration. Collaboration is often a natural outgrowth of working together in a remote retreat setting. Sgroi and Saltiel (1998) wrote, "The power of a collaborative partnership is derived from the synergy created when human beings connect in productive, meaningful activity" (p. 87). In discussing collaboration, Sgroi and Saltiel name many of the same elements that are key in community building: deep trust and respect, shared goal or purpose, complementary but different (collaborative partners), and synergy between partners. Furthermore, successful partners select each other. In a retreat setting the groups do not select one another; in fact, many in the groups never met one another before. But retreat settings are conducive to making new friends, forming partnerships during activities, and creating long-term support networks. Sgroi and Saltiel go on to say, "The potential and power of collaborative partnerships is the power of humanity. It is the power of human touch, the life force emitted and exchanged between human beings through physical, intellectual, and emotional pathways. We give energy and life to one another. This is at the heart of understanding the power of collaborative partnerships" (p. 91).

Another interesting aspect of collaborative learning and learning in community is that the process is as important as the content. Saltiel (1998) states, "There is magic in a collaborative partnership. It provides the power to transform ordinary learning experiences into dynamic relationships, resulting in a synergistic process of accomplishment" (p. 5).

As one participant said: "Most of all, I treasure the depth of sharing that comes from being together, in a common way, on the boat, at the table, in the woods, hiking, studying, and sleeping. Trust and appreciation grows among us. As people tell personal stories, emotions are stirred and rare insights are passed along. Everyone begins to feel that we are a phenomenon of connection to a larger picture of education and humanity" (Ann Wing Quest, personal communication with the authors, 2000).

Catalysts for Change. A beautiful and vibrant retreat setting, a warm feeling of community, and multisensory experiences act as catalysts for change. The dynamics among learners and the supportive environment woo learners to change. Perhaps it is a positive "disorienting dilemma" that pushes people out of their comfort zones, creates an atmosphere where there is a willingness to take risks. Being completely away from the usual demands and constraints of life allows one to think outside the box. Time and again, participants are allowed to reflect creatively and freely about what they desire; they are allowed to discover their passions. Dialogue and discourse between learners leads them to cooperative inquiry. Out-of-classroom learning among the participants leads to an energy and desire to work toward healing others and social activism. "The grandeur of the Alaskan scenery creates a spiritual sensibility that forms a context for learning that prompts one to avoid the trivial and make the awareness of the profound more available for reflection and meaning. To live together for three days in such a magnificent locale deepens the learning because there are few distractions, and students and teachers alike can immerse themselves continuously in what they find to be relevant. With learning as the focus, they can literally harness the majestic in service of the birth of new knowledge" (Raymond Wlodkowski, personal communication, 2000).

Conclusion

In this chapter, we outlined experiences on Yukon Island as an example of the formation of learning communities in remote retreat settings. There are opportunities for direct transference to other settings and remote locations. When planning a course or workshop in a remote setting it is important to consider the learning environment, the building of community, and the learning process. As one participant said: "Being a part of a residential learning community such as Yukon Island significantly expanded my appreciation of the adult learning process, adult educators, nature, and the incredible camaraderie that takes place among peers when they are allowed to freely share knowledge, perspectives, living space, and collaborative skills in order to reach common goals. This was a learning experience that was not only transformative, but for me, nearly spiritual. Collectively, this is what the program at Yukon Island is all about" (De Bora McIntosh, personal communication, 2000).

Sessions in remote retreat settings may not be for everyone. Some learners are reluctant to take the risk of going into the unknown or living a primitive lifestyle. Those who do take the risk feel rewarded by their accomplishment. Having said this, there might be no better place to build community. Such remote settings foster collaboration, promote risk taking, and build trust; there is greater equity between facilitators and learners. People feel free to learn in a natural setting.

Although the goals of the classes that take place on the island are centered on an educational course or theme, the ideas people come up with during the course, the relationships that form or deepen, and the dreams that are expressed have a way of continuing to persist and develop long after the program is over.

One participant said: "Back in Homer after the weekend on the island, as I fueled up my car with the rain pouring down, a raven landed on my windshield and then stood on my hood while I filled my gas tank. The raven talked to me, cocking its head from side to side, and took small prancing steps close to me as if to say, 'You're going to be fine. Welcome home.' I am Tlingit, Raven moiety, Coho clan, and that raven reaffirmed the spiritual weekend I had had" (Barbara Fleek, personal communication with the authors, 2000).

The learners' descriptions of their experiences speak to the importance of learning communities in retreat settings. Each part of the world has beautiful places; it is for the facilitators of learning to seek out these settings. "At places like Yukon Island hidden passions reveal themselves; people find focus and experience transformation. Courses held in natural settings go far beyond measurement by any academic standard, because the value is unique and personal for every individual. I believe that it is in places like these that commitment to serve is born" (Ann Wing Quest, personal communication with the authors, 2000).

References

Andrews, L. "Earth, Body, and Spirit." In R. Carson and B. Shield (eds.), *Handbook for the Soul.* New York: Little Brown, 1995.

Apps, J. *Mastering the Teaching of Adults.* Malabar, Fla.: Krieger, 1991.

American Heritage Dictionary (3rd ed.). Boston: Houghton Mifflin, 1992.

Cousineau, P. "Soulfulness Is a Verb." In R. Carson and B. Shield (eds.), *Handbook for the Soul.* New York: Little Brown, 1995.

Edelson, P. "Creativity and Adult Education." In P. Edelson and P. Malone (eds.), *Enhancing Creativity in Adult and Continuing Education: Innovative Approaches, Methods, and Ideas.* New Directions for Adult and Continuing Education, no. 81. San Francisco: Jossey-Bass, 1999.

Palmer, P. *The Courage to Teach: Exploring the Inner Landscape of a Teacher's Life.* San Francisco: Jossey-Bass, 1998.

Saltiel, I. "Defining Collaborative Partnerships." In I. Saltiel, A. Sgroi, and R. Brockett (eds.), *The Power and Potential of Collaborative Learning Partnerships.* New Directions for Adult and Continuing Education, no. 79. San Francisco: Jossey-Bass, 1998.

Sgroi, A., and Saltiel, I. "Human Connections." In I. Saltiel, A. Sgroi, and R. Brockett (eds.), *The Power and Potential of Collaborative Learning Partnerships.* New Directions for Adult and Continuing Education, no. 79. San Francisco: Jossey-Bass, 1998.

GRETCHEN T. BERSCH is professor emeritus at the University of Alaska-Anchorage, where she is a coordinator in the adult education graduate program.

CAROLE L. LUND is adjunct professor of adult education and program adviser for student programs at the University of Alaska-Anchorage.

7

Cohort groups in adult and higher education programs provide the skills needed to build and maintain learning communities, which are needed for healthy and sustainable societies.

A Small Circle of Friends: Cohort Groups as Learning Communities

Randee Lipson Lawrence

This chapter looks at cohort learning groups in higher education. A *cohort* is defined here as a small group of learners who complete an entire program of study as a single unit. The chapter begins with a discussion of how these groups create and sustain community. Co-creating knowledge through collaborative learning and experiential knowing is identified as an important outcome of cohort learning. Communication, interdependence, shared responsibility, power, democracy, and conflict are examined as part of the community process. Peer networks and ways the community is maintained outside of the classroom are discussed. On-line communities are examined to illustrate how emerging technologies can assist or inhibit our connection. The chapter concludes with a discussion of the potential of cohorts to extend learning and influence larger communities.

Holding Communal Space: The Circle

In higher education programs, participants usually enter cohort groups as strangers to one another connected only through a mutual desire to complete a program of study. Although forming a learning community may not be their primary reason for choosing the program, most come with an expectation and willingness to work collaboratively.

A group of individuals with a common goal does not automatically constitute a community. Communities develop over time and with intention. Members of the community must come to know each other and develop a respect for one another's strengths, weaknesses, similarities, and differences. When commitment is high and contributions from all members are valued, communities have the potential to co-create knowledge, make effective decisions, and effect change.

The circle has come to be almost synonymous with adult education. Chairs are arranged in a circle to promote free-flowing dialogue and democratic process. The concept of the circle, however, goes much deeper than an arrangement of furniture. Forming a circle is an ancient ritual. Our ancestors gathered in a circle around a fire for warmth and to cook the food that was provided by groups of hunters and gatherers. The circle provided the basis for socialization, decision making, and problem solving (Baldwin, 1994). Baldwin teaches about "circle consciousness" (p. 230) to groups and organizations of all types. The concept of "holding the rim" means that all members of the community are responsible for the whole. If a member is struggling, the other group members will hold up the rim and offer whatever kind of assistance is needed.

One way the circle or community spirit can be fostered in a cohort is through a residential learning experience at the start of the program. Students come together for a period of time to focus on their studies and build relationships with those with whom they will be traveling along their educational journey. Separated from work, family, and daily responsibilities, participants have the luxury of totally immersing themselves in the experience. When they share meals, sleeping quarters, and daily activities it helps them form intimate bonds in a short period of time. Living closely with others in this way, facades are dropped and authentic knowing is fostered. Opportunities for informal learning occur through spontaneous conversations, on walks, during meals, on porch steps, in pubs, and in people's rooms late into the night (Lawrence, 1999a).

Cohort groups that do not have the opportunity for a residential experience can develop as a community through intentional activities early in the life of the cohort. A class on group process can help students look more intentionally at the dynamics of their learning group. Ultimately, being together over an extended period of time helps establish the community. Students do not have to start the process of getting acquainted over again for each new class. A comfort level is achieved as they get to know one another at deeper levels, which allows for more intimate dialogue. Fear of failure or "looking stupid" is reduced as they learn what they can expect from their peers. This comfort level often results in more risk taking and self-disclosure.

Once the community has formed, strong bonds develop. Participants feel a sense of loss if one member withdraws from the community or does not participate in a significant event. When a member is absent from class it not only results in a loss for the absent member but also deprives the others of that person's contribution.

Co-Creativity: Weaving Knowledge Webs

Collaborative learning—defined as students and teachers engaged in a process of mutual inquiry and reflection through the sharing of ideas, experiences, and perspectives—is at the core of the cohort model. It involves exploring problems and issues through dialogue from the multiple viewpoints of the participants in order to arrive at a deeper understanding. In collaborative learning groups, participants learn from their peers, teach their teachers, and create knowledge together (Lawrence, 1996). Participants learn not only from each other's knowledge but from their own questions and their own areas of confusion.

N.F.S. Gruntvig, founder of the Danish folk schools, used this teaching practice as early as 1832. He advocated a process of "reciprocal teaching," where students and teachers engaged in an ongoing dialogue that allowed them to gain insights into themselves and their world (Warren, 1989).

Dialogue in an adult education context often involves the participants in sharing personal stories of their lived experiences. In a cohort, these stories tend to take on more meaning over time as the community develops and matures. As participants recount their experiences, others listen, interpret, give feedback, and relate similar experiences. These experiences become the text for learning as multiple perspectives are shared and understanding is deepened.

In addition to sharing experiences in a cohort group, members learn through the *baking of ideas* (Mealman and Lawrence, 1998). As they develop a comfort level with one another over time, they are more willing to risk throwing out half-baked, not fully formed ideas for consideration. These ideas are discussed, affirmed, built on, challenged, debated, and ultimately "baked" through collaborative effort. The community members have shared ownership in the knowledge created.

In cohort learning groups, the knowledge that is co-created is greater than the sum of each individual member's knowledge. Whipple (1987) believes that in collaborative learning groups, there is a distinct knowledge represented by the collective in addition to the knowledge of each member of the group. I have found that the synergy created by cohort groups actually represents multiple knowledges. People interact with one another in various configurations of smaller groups, which create group knowledge too. Their knowledge serves as an additional ingredient for the collaborative pot, which results in a richer and spicier mixture. Because knowledge is never static, the taste is continually changing as new recipes are invented.

Discourse Communities: Holding the Rim

In a learning community, all participants are responsible for the growth and well-being of every member. Therefore, actions by individuals affect the entire community. Helping out a classmate helps the group—not just the individual—to succeed. At the same time, failure to carry out one's assigned task adversely affects the entire group. Cohorts foster a spirit of cooperation by involving the members in collaborative decision making. Beyond the formal structures of participative governance and group project teams, members hold up the rim by freely sharing their time and expertise with others. They recognize that individual success depends on the success of the collective. Most cohorts develop a culture of cooperation and caring as opposed to competition. If a member is having difficulty grasping course concepts, peers will often share their papers, or spend time discussing ideas and perspectives.

One advantage of learning in a group is that there is less chance an individual will give up when going through a difficult period. If a member is considering dropping out of the group, for example, the others tend to rally round and do everything in their power to retain the individual in the community. Keeping the community intact is a priority. Because communities are made up of individuals, this commitment extends to each individual member. This cooperative spirit is essential to the health of the cohort.

Cohort members are parts of a whole. As individuals, they take on different roles that can facilitate or hinder the group process. They serve important and necessary functions, from keeping the group on-task to providing comic relief when tensions are high. A cohort is a minisociety. In a society, people take on the roles of shopkeeper, teacher, healer, spiritual leader, and so on. These interdependent roles are necessary for the community to function. A cohort, like any group, is made up of individuals with different strengths and weaknesses. All members contribute in different ways. They may be group leader, recorder, content expert, philosopher, comic, and so on.

As the cohort continues together through several courses, there are multiple opportunities for leadership. At various points during the program, almost everyone assumes a leadership role. Horton (1990) described this flow of leadership when he articulated his vision of his Highlander Folk School as a large tapestry of many colors. "During various periods, different colors would dominate over others. At times one color would be wide or become narrow or even fade out. Some colors, however, have always been present in the tapestry. New colors are continually added and old colors reappear" (p. 134). Over time, students learn to take on different roles and experiment with different ways of being, using their peers as models. Quieter members tend to become more vocal, and more dominant members learn to listen.

The role of the instructor in the cohort learning community is critical. He or she is a catalyst for nurturing group development and cohesiveness. The instructor is responsible for creating a safe environment for learning, providing opportunities for group interaction, encouraging critical reflection, giving feedback, modeling respect, and fostering independence. After setting the stage the instructor needs to step back and allow the community to develop in a natural way. This may take the form of intentionally remaining silent, allowing the group members to grapple with ideas on their own, thus creating a "horizontal information flow" (Kubayashi, 1994, p. 234). A group of peers are less likely to see one member's contribution as the only correct answer than they would if a perceived authority figure provided it. They are more willing to consider multiple perspectives, which leads to knowledge construction through social interaction.

At first glance, critical, feminist, and liberatory educators may be seen to view the classroom as a democratic space where students and teachers have an equal share of the power. Yet in the academy that is never entirely possible. As long as faculty are responsible for course objectives and evaluation and are accountable to the accrediting bodies, they maintain authority. Even in classrooms where students are encouraged to develop their own objectives and engage in self-evaluation and peer evaluation, the instructor continues to influence the group in subtle, and sometimes not so subtle, ways.

Collaborative learning challenges traditional notions of the instructor's authority in the classroom (Bruffee, 1993). As students are organized into collaborative groups and engaged in the process of teaching and learning from one another, the teacher's authority is often called into question. Many students are uncomfortable with accepting a share of the authority or granting it to a peer. According to Bruffee there is a process of *reacculturation* that is necessary before students will accept a share in the authority that is needed for collaboration to occur.

Participants often describe their cohort as being like a family. Like families, cohorts can be both functional and dysfunctional. In most families, people can express negative emotions without fear of rejection. However, even in caring, supportive families, the members do not always get along and conflict occurs. Conflicts in cohorts are often caused by misunderstanding, power imbalance, or a lack of tolerance of perspectives stemming from differing worldviews. Although familiarity with one's classmates is usually an asset to the learning community, familiarity can sometimes lead to "automatic vision" (Lawrence and Mealman, 1996, p. 35), where an individual assumes that he or she knows the meaning of a classmate's words or actions and gives them only cursory consideration.

Belenky, Clinchy, Goldberger, and Tarule (1997) found that groups worked out their differences much like members of a family do. Because they "knew each other's quirks" (p. 120), they could devise strategies for working with those individuals and for resolving their conflicts.

Theater in the Round: Behind the Scenes

The learning community created by the cohort group is not confined to the hours a class is in session or the space that defines the classroom. Community activity continues beyond the spatial and temporal environment. Participants communicate in between classes by telephone or e-mail and in face-to-face gatherings. They use these informal times to explore ideas and threads that they are not sure about. They know that they will get validation to continue in the same direction or assistance in rethinking the idea. Without the threat of grades or other evaluative constructs, students are often more willing to step outside their own perspective to consider each other's views. Much significant learning occurs during these informal times, which include class break periods and after-class gatherings at a local bar or coffee shop. According to one participant, "The bar is where everything else happens." Students often leave class full of ideas and emotions. They need a way to process this stimulus before returning to their homes. In these informal settings, ideas are born, feelings are expressed, and knots of confusion are untied. Freed from the need to "perform" or look intelligent, more creative energy can flow. These are also the places where conflicts and differences between members get worked out. Sometimes interaction outside of class is precipitated by a crisis or conflict such as one group experienced when a new instructor alienated many of the class members. They refused to let the group fall apart and used collective action to resolve the conflict. This was a significant learning experience for the group. As one member put it, "It forced us to question our own value system: What do I (we) believe in?"

Interaction often goes well beyond the content of the course and engages the whole person. Students in cohorts tend to form informal resource networks to assist one another. They share expertise such as computer or graphic arts skills or instructional strategies, as well as books and Internet resources, and help one another explore new careers and target job leads. They support one another emotionally and provide assistance in times of personal crisis.

Saturn's Rings: Cyberspace Communities

Learning groups do not need to meet face-to-face to form a community. Over the last decade, undergraduate and graduate degree programs are increasingly being offered entirely on-line. This section focuses on on-line programs that are asynchronous and cohort-based, and create their own learning communities in much the same way as the face-to-face groups that have been discussed.

On-line learning by nature requires a certain degree of autonomy and self-direction. The learners "attend class" alone with their computers. Yet it is the sense of being a part of a community that sustains the learning group. According to Palloff and Pratt (1999), a collaborative environment with equal participation by all is essential to the survival of the on-line learning group. Although some believe it is possible to maintain a successful on-line learning community in the absence of any face-to-face interaction, my experience suggests that bringing the students together for a residential workshop at the onset of their program goes a long way to promote community

(Lawrence, 1999b). Participants get to know one another and have a face, voice, and memories of shared experiences to relate to the name on the screen.

In an on-line course, students do not have the option of having coffee together during break or going out for a beer after class. They need to find more creative ways to sustain their virtual community. One way this happens is through a virtual class lounge. This is an on-line space where participants share aspects of their lives that transcend the course material. They tell stories of family and work life, seek and offer advice, post resources such as interesting Web sites, celebrate successes, and provide support and encouragement. They also use the lounge as a place to share aspects of themselves that may not be revealed during class discussions. Sometimes digital photos are posted to communicate what words cannot. Although instructors are often welcome in the lounge, they do not facilitate or control discussions that take place there. This is especially important because the cohort remains intact while the instructors rotate in and out. Students who participate in the residential workshops find that they develop community-building skills that they continue to use on-line. As one participant said, "We continually organize ourselves within each thread, sharing information, reflecting, asking each other questions, giving feedback, validating and encouraging each other."

Although many of the dynamics of building and sustaining a learning community are similar in on-line and face-to-face cohorts, the communication patterns tend to differ on-line. One advantage of on-line asynchronous communication is that no one can be interrupted. This gives the quieter, more introspective members time to complete their thoughts before being cut off, or worse, silenced by more dominant members. These skills can be translated to other communities. Participants find they spend more time thinking through ideas before speaking, which allows for more thoughtful, reflective comments. Silence also takes on a very different meaning. In an on-line community, members are dependent on the participation of others. In the absence of nonverbal cues, it is difficult to know what silence means. If one makes a comment and no one responds, the participant is left wondering whether he or she is being ignored, whether the message was unclear, or whether anyone is actually out there. It is also easier to misinterpret comments that are solely text-based. Participants need to work harder to keep the community functional.

The instructor working with the on-line cohort needs to know when to comment and when to let the group take over. If an instructor makes frequent comments, the students tend to have a dialogue with the instructor rather than each other and some of the community feeling breaks down. If comments are made in an authoritative way, the students may perceive that there is no room for disagreement and further conversation may be thwarted. To facilitate an on-line community effectively, the instructor needs to set the stage by providing opportunities for participants to get to know one another and share in the facilitation of group discussions, pose provocative questions, and then get out of the way.

Because on-line learning has yet to become the standard in most institutions, most students in such groups have no previous experience being a part of an on-line community. They soon realize that they are learning how to become a community, experientially. There is no other way. "You soon realize that to learn to play you have to play to learn" (Turkle, 1995, p. 70). The learners most often retain this experiential knowledge because it becomes a part of them.

As the benefits of on-line learning are realized, more and more traditional classes are incorporating some components of on-line learning, including class listservs and discussion forums to communicate between classes and for small group work. Students post papers on-line for peer critique and use the Web to connect with larger communities.

Concentric Circles: Extending the Community

Cohort learning groups in higher education are finite. They formally end when the degree program is completed. Yet the community often continues well beyond the formal part of the program. Some groups continue to meet informally for months or even years after graduation. Although they value the socialization and friendship, their needs for continued affiliation may be intellectual as well. They realize that they enjoy learning together and from each other and that they want to hang onto those learning opportunities. Students realize that they have formed bonds that do not exist in other communities. Their shared experiences, projects, dialogues, and so on cannot be appreciated in the same way by others. They become used to regular intellectual stimulation with like-minded peers and feel a void when that is no longer occurring. I know of one group that is still meeting after more than two years. They get together about once a month to plan an educational event, which may include a dialogue, guest speaker, or field trip. Motivation to attend these sessions is high, and most make an effort to be there.

The learning about forming and sustaining community is not limited to the confines of the cohort group. It expands exponentially as members use the knowledge in their roles as members of other communities. One participant said the experience "doesn't just affect you. It affects everyone around you, who affects everyone around them, and then it grows." Cohort members realize that developing community takes considerable effort; it does not happen automatically. They look for people with similar passions. They consciously take what they have learned and bring it to their place of business, place of worship, and neighborhood. They help others to develop community by organizing participative decision-making groups. They take with them the confidence to challenge the status quo as a collective rather than as an individual. After their struggles in learning to listen to and be respectful of others, they take away the collaborative skills of paying attention, valuing the contributions of others, and sharing ideas. They encourage their students and colleagues to bring in knowledge and resources to share and facilitate discussions to create collaborative knowledge.

One cohort participant came up with a metaphor to describe this process of extending community. She saw her group as a grove of trees with shared or intertwined roots. The branches of the trees were now spread out in many different directions. This metaphor could be expanded as the trees bore fruit. Some of the seeds might drop to the ground and sprout seedlings. Some might be blown further afield by the wind or carried off by squirrels to be dropped and take root in other places. And so the community continues.

Implications for Lifelong Learning

We do not exist as individuals in isolation. Humankind's survival is dependent on our ability to form community with others. Cohort participants not only form community in their small groups but become part of a larger community, the community of scholars. They seek out new opportunities for discourse after their formal program ends.

Learning communities are sustained by interdependence, a willingness to be changed, and a deep sense of commitment. This chapter concludes with a story that illustrates this kind of commitment.

Patty, age fifty, was a member of a master's degree cohort that was nearing completion. For their culminating project, the group chose to construct a day-and-a-half-long conference, where they would be the primary presenters. They spent the last three months of the program preparing for the event. Four days before the conference, Patty began experiencing symptoms of disorientation and short-term memory loss. A consultation with a doctor revealed that she had a brain tumor. Immediate surgery was recommended. Patty looked at her doctor in disbelief. "But you don't understand!" she exclaimed. "I'm in a master's program!" Patty attended the weekend conference with her cohort peers, and on the following Tuesday she underwent successful surgery for her tumor.

The cohort group offers an opportunity to develop skills in communication, accountability, respect, love, conflict resolution, and commitment. Cohorts foster collective knowledge and wisdom that sustain us as thoughtful and active participants in our world.

References

Baldwin, C. *Calling the Circle*. Newburg, Ore.: Swan Raven, 1994.
Belenky, M. F., Clinchy, B. M., Goldberger, N. R., and Tarule, J. M. *Women's Ways of Knowing: The Development of Self, Voice, and Mind*. New York: Basic Books, 1997. (Originally published 1986.)

Bruffee, K. A. *Collaborative Learning, Higher Education, Interdependence, and the Authority of Knowledge.* Baltimore: Johns Hopkins University Press, 1993.

Horton, M. *The Long Haul.* New York: Doubleday, 1990.

Kubayashi, Y. "Conceptual Acquisition and Change Through Social Interaction." *Human Development,* 1994, *37*(4), 233–241.

Lawrence, R. L. "Co-Learning Communities: A Hermeneutic Account of Adult Learning in Higher Education Through the Lived World of Cohorts." Unpublished doctoral dissertation, Northern Illinois University, 1996.

Lawrence, R. L. "Transcending Boundaries: Building Community Through Residential Adult Learning." *Proceedings of the Eighteenth Annual Midwest Research-to-Practice Conference in Adult, Continuing, and Community Education,* Saint Louis, Mo., pp. 173–179, 1999a. (ED 442 323)

Lawrence, R. L. "Cohorts in Cyberspace: Creating Community Online." *Proceedings of the Nineteenth Annual Alliance–ACE Conference,* Sarasota Springs, N.Y., pp. 95–100, 1999b. (ED 447 269)

Lawrence, R. L., and Mealman, C. A. "Seizing Learning Opportunities: Embracing a Collaborative Process." *Proceedings of the Sixteenth Annual Alliance–ACE Conference,* St. Pete Beach, Fla., pp. 29–51, 1996. (ED 402 511)

Mealman, C. A., and Lawrence, R. L. "Co-Creating Knowledge: A Collaborative Inquiry into Collaborative Inquiry." *Proceedings of the Seventeenth Annual Midwest Research-to-Practice Conference in Adult, Continuing, and Community Education,* Muncie, Ind., pp. 133–138, 1998. (ED 424 419)

Palloff, R. M., and Pratt, K. *Building Learning Communities in Cyberspace: Effective Strategies for the On-Line Classroom.* San Francisco: Jossey-Bass, 1999.

Turkle, S. *Life on the Screen: Identity in the Age of the Internet.* New York: Simon & Schuster, 1995.

Warren, C. "Andragogy and N.F.S. Gruntvig: A Critical Link." *Adult Education Quarterly,* 1989, *39*(4), 211–223.

Whipple, W. R. "Collaborative Learning: Recognizing It When We See It." *AAHE Bulletin,* Oct. 1987, 1–6.

RANDEE LIPSON LAWRENCE *is associate professor of adult and continuing education at National-Louis University in Chicago.*

Learning in community takes a variety of forms and generally emphasizes the community rather than the individual level of learning. Although many learning communities are homogeneous in nature, power and politics play a role, and the presence of a facilitator can change the dynamics.

8

Adult Learning in Community: Themes and Threads

David S. Stein, Susan Imel

Adults are creating learning spaces outside of formal educational boundaries. Learning is occurring in naturally forming communities around educational, environmental, social, and civic life situations. Learning communities are developing when ordinary people desire to control everyday life events and come to know these events through a learning process. In a learning community, a space is created where a diversity of views and ideas can be shared and honored and sustainable relationships formed, although power relationships and politics may create barriers to learning. Through learning communities, participants create the content, develop learning approaches, and situate learning in a specific context. Learning in community can produce a shared sense of purpose, a sense of belonging to a group that welcomes differences as a means to understand a local situation better (Wheatley, 1998). Learning is celebrated and seen as a vehicle for citizens to build more life-sustaining places to live, work, and enjoy (Longworth, 1999). By participating in a learning community, citizens actively confront issues and move toward a common future (Sussmuth, 1998).

The type of learning that occurs in community emphasizes the social or communal as opposed to the individual (Barab and Duffy, 2000; Heaney, 1995; Wenger, 1998; Zukas and Malcolm, 2000). Theories that focus on the social nature of cognition and meaning—as opposed to individual learning—are stressed (Barab and Duffy, 2000), and the learning is situated in the social context (Hansman, 2001). The work of Lave and Wenger (1991) is the basis for much of the writing about the social nature of learning. In this type of learning, "students and teachers are considered to be social and cultural actors with identities emerging from their wider social experiences" (Zukas and Malcolm, 2000, p. 6), and the process and the content of learning are intertwined (Heaney, 1995; Senge, 1997; Zukas and Malcolm, 2000).

Common Themes in Learning Communities

This volume has attempted to explore a variety of meanings for and experiences in learning in community. But in all the stories presented, a number of themes and threads emerge.

Place Is Important. First, adult learners voluntarily create learning spaces related to the time and place in which problems are situated. The authors in this volume have described different places for communities to form that allow the members to engage with each other on specific concerns. Bersch and Lund (Chapter Six), in describing remote retreat learning, and Lawrence (Chapter Seven), in portraying cohort learning, show how environment and experience can interact to produce shared insights about graduate study. The space itself becomes an element in producing learning. Stein (Chapter Two), in describing the formation of the Community Futures 2010 committee, and Imel and Zengler (Chapter Three), in discussing collaborative interagency teams, show how learning spaces emerge in organizational and community settings. The learning space is neutral with respect to the various segments represented in the learning effort. The neutrality of the space is "owned" by the learning community that fosters learning.

Learning Content Relates to the Community's Daily Life. A second theme is that learning in community produces content situated in the daily life concerns of the members. The experience of learning in a community creates collective knowledge owned by the members. As Hugo suggests in Chapter One, it serves as "a laboratory of adults' life concerns." The process of learning in community produces community wisdom because the knowledge is applied to improve daily life activities or for seeking insights about the social and intellectual world (Elias and Merriam, 1995). Learning is cooperative, purposeful, and designed to strengthen a group's ability to learn from and apply wisdom to everyday life situations. The text shows that the content produced from learning in community has social and political dimensions based on the ability of the learning group to apply power to bring about changes in their interests. Whereas Stein (Chapter Two) and Imel and Zengler (Chapter Three) show that groups may use research data to reflect the interests of the public who are not represented in the group, Owenby (Chapter Four) suggests that the content produced may be influenced by organizational interests rather than be generated through the group's actual encounters with situations. Owenby further discusses the tension between the voluntary nature of learning in community and a forced learning situation and the learning produced by the group. In Chapter Five,

Drennon describes how power relationships and politics can affect the democratic nature of a learning community. It should be noted that the cases presented in the sourcebook have a strong educational and class bias. The participants discussed in the cases are primarily middle class.

Knowledge Is Locally Produced. A third theme of learning in community is that it encourages citizens to produce local knowledge. In most chapters, the members of the learning community learn by active engagement and are directly affected by the outcomes of defining a problem, collecting data, interpreting the data, and formulating actions based on their shared understanding of the situation (Lacy, 2001). Learning in community is learning *with* others, more than learning from or about others (Heron, 1996). However, for the interagency teams discussed by Imel and Zengler (Chapter Three), learning about each other formed the basis for the group learning to occur. In most of the learning communities described in the volume, the expertise of an adult education facilitator is limited or absent. In a learning community, knowledge is created by the group, shared with the group, and arises from the interactions of the group with a common situation. As suggested by Bersch and Lund (Chapter Six) and Stein (Chapter Two), the facilitator may become a co-learner. Instructional leadership changes as the need for specific information or skills may arise. Expertise is located in the group's shared insights and in individual members' experiences. Although learning in community might be considered a form of informal collaborative learning (Marsick and Volpe, 1999; Saltiel, Sgroi, and Brockett, 1998), the learning is intentional and is in response to situations requiring an action at the personal, organizational, and community levels. Learning in community makes the knowledge gained explicit rather than tacit. Using empirically obtained data, or through reflection on experiences, the members of the learning community understand how to improve an aspect of their situation.

Learning Communities May Be Powerful Structures. A fourth theme is that a learning community may be a "power structure with which to reckon" (Hugo, Chapter One). The use of the term *community* can mask the privileging of homogeneity because many communities focus on common interests and bonds (St. Clair, 1998). The power issues inherent in learning communities are made explicit by Owenby (Chapter Four) and Drennon (Chapter Five). Both of these authors consider the importance of the psychological and social environment of learning communities, including how a learning community reflects the power and politics of the broader society in which it is located.

The Challenge for Adult Educators

The authors in this volume have shown that learning in community is a form of learning where adults voluntarily agree to learn about and take action on some aspects of their communal situation. Hugo (Chapter One) views learning communities as learning laboratories where adults can come together based on their experiences with real issues, gain new knowledge, access community resources coordinated for the benefits of their learning, and take action as a result of their learning. By learning in community, adults create a temporal space for constructing individual and collective knowledge; they develop rules for exchanging ideas, data, and solutions. As Lawrence describes it (Chapter Seven), the learning community may assume an identity beyond that of each of its original members. As Imel and Zengler (Chapter Three) and Lawrence (Chapter Seven) point out, it may even continue as members enter and exit the space over time. Thus, the collective learning remains in the community.

The notion of learning in community poses a challenge for professional adult educators. As the chapters show, learning in community is a tool used by individuals to deal with local issues. Hugo (Chapter One) and Stein (Chapter Two) both acknowledge the tension that exists between the public educating itself and adult education practitioners educating the public, and Drennon (Chapter Five) describes many issues and challenges for those in the role of facilitator. The challenge for the adult educator is to encourage formation of learning communities without interfering in the learning that occurs or using their expert knowledge to direct the group in its struggle to learn.

References

Barab, S. A., and Duffy, T. M. "From Practice Fields to Communities of Practice." In D. H. Jonassen and S. M. Land (eds.), *Theoretical Foundations of Learning*. Hillsdale, N.J.: Erlbaum, 2000.

Elias, J., and Merriam, S. *Philosophical Foundations of Adult Education*. Malabar: Fla., 1995.

Hansman, C. A. "Context-Based Adult Learning." In S. B. Merrian (ed.), *The New Update on Adult Learning Theory*. New Directions for Adult and Continuing Education, no. 89. San Francisco: Jossey-Bass, 2001.

Heaney, T. "Learning to Control Democratically: Ethical Questions in Situated Adult Education." Unpublished paper, June 1995. (ED 397 238)

Heron, J. *Cooperative Inquiry: Research into the Human Condition*. Thousand Oaks, Calif.: Sage, 1996.

Lacy, W. "Democratizing Science in an Era of Expert and Private Knowledge." *Higher Education Exchange,* 2001, *1,* 52–61.

Lave, J., and Wenger, E. *Situated Learning: Legitimate Peripheral Participation*. New York: Cambridge University Press, 1991.

Longworth, N. *Making Lifelong Learning Work: Learning Cities for a Learning Century*. London: Kogan Page, 1999.

Marsick, V., and Volpe, M. "The Nature and Need for Informal Learning." In V. Marsick and M. Volpe (eds.), *Informal Learning on the Job: Advances in Developing Human Resources*. San Francisco: Berrett-Koehler, 1999.

Saltiel, I., Sgroi, A., and Brockett, R. (eds.). *The Power and Potential of Collaborative Learning Partnerships*. New Directions for Adult and Continuing Education, no. 79. San Francisco: Jossey-Bass, 1998.

Senge, P. M. "Creating Learning Communities." *Executive Excellence,* Mar. 1997, *15*(3), 17–18.

St. Clair, R. "On the Commonplace: Reclaiming Community in Adult Education." *Adult Education Quarterly*, 1998, *49*(1), 5–14.

Sussmuth, R. "The Future-Capability of Society." In F. Hesselbein, M. Goldsmith, R. Beckhard, and R. Schubert (eds.), *The Community of the Future*. San Francisco: Jossey-Bass, 1998.

Wenger, E. *Communities of Practice: Learning, Meaning, and Identity*. New York: Cambridge University Press, 1998.

Wheatley, M., and Kellner-Rogers, M. "The Paradox and Promise of Community." In F. Hesselbein, M. Goldsmith, R. Beckhard, and R. Schubert (eds.), *The Community of the Future*. San Francisco: Jossey-Bass, 1998.

Zukas, M., and Malcolm, J. "Pedagogies for Lifelong Learning: Building Bridges or Building Walls?" Working Papers of the Global Colloquium on Supporting Lifelong Learning [online], Milton Keynes, U.K.: Open University, 2000 [http://www. open.ac.uk/lifelong-learning].

DAVID S. STEIN *is associate professor of adult education and workforce development at The Ohio State University, College of Education.*

SUSAN IMEL *is senior research specialist at the Center on Education and Training for Employment, The Ohio State University, College of Education.*

INDEX

Addams, J., 15
Adler, M., 16
Adult educators: challenge for, 95–96; role in cohort learning community, 86–87; as "servants of scholarship"/"creators of national intelligence," 16
Adult learning communities: cohort groups as, 83–91; common themes in, 94–95; cyberspace, 88–90; definitional concerns of, 6–7; evidence of usable past of, 9–10; as historic adult education theme, 5–6; historiographic issues of, 6–10; history shaping understanding of, 10–12; nature of learning in, 93–94; organizational, 51–58; remote retreat settings for, 73–81; social movements and, 18–21. *See also* Community; Learning
Adult learning community themes: knowledge is locally produced, 95; learning content relates to community, 94–95; place is important, 94; as powerful structures, 95
Alinsky, S., 18
Alonso, H. H., 18
Altrichter, H., 61
American Association for Adult Education, 13
American Heritage Dictionary, 78
Andrews, L., 75
Apps, J., 73
Autonomous community learning groups, 12–14

Barab, S. A., 93
Barber, E., 32
Belenky, M. F., 22, 87
Belzer, A., 61
Bender, T., 7, 8, 9, 10, 18, 21
Bersch, G. T., 73, 81, 94, 95
Bitterman, J., 13, 17
Bond, L., 22
Borstein, D., 9
Bowling Alone: The Collapse and Revival of American Community (Putnam), 10
Brockett, R., 95

Brookfield, S., 5, 9, 12, 14, 16, 17, 21
Bruffee, K. A., 87
Buckeye County, 36
Buckeye County future images workshop, 33
Buckeye County Health Department, 28, 30, 32
Buckingham, M., 54, 56
Burnaby, B., 21
Byrn Mawr Summer Schools for Women Workers, 19

Caffarella, R. S., 45, 46
Camino, L., 32
Campaigning, 34
Campbell, P., 21
Carnegie Corporation, 16
Carr, W., 61
Cassidy, A., 29
Catholic worker movement, 19
Cervero, R. M., 53, 54, 65, 66
Chrisman, N., 32
Ciske, S., 32
Clark, S., 19
Clinchy, B. M., 67, 87
Cochran-Smith, M., 68, 69
Coffman, C., 54, 56
Cohort learning community: behind-the-scenes activities of, 87–88; in cyberspace, 88–90; as discourse communities, 85–87; extending/expanding, 90–91; forming communal space in, 83–84; implications for lifelong learning, 91; role of instructor in, 86–87
Collaboration: Common Good successful use of, 42–44; used in remote retreat settings, 79
Committing, 31–33
Common Good local linkage teams (LLTs), 42, 43–44, 46–48
Common Good (Ohio): collaboration used for success of, 42–44; communities of practice in, 46–47; connecting practice to theory, 45–48; goal of, 41–42; learning connection in, 44–45; learning organizations in, 47–48

Common Good one-stop centers, 43
Communicating, 35–36
Communities of practice, 46–47
Community: autonomous learning groups in, 12–14; community action groups in, 18–21; community development groups in, 14–18; connecting learning to social change in, 37; dominant yet distorted conceptions of, 7–9; *gemeinschaft* (community)-*gesellschaft* (society) continuum, 7, 8, 21; as "laboratories for learning," 17; participation in learning in community by, 29–31; relationship between adult learning and, 10–12; relationship between learning and, 5–6; relationship between learning content and, 94–95; three historical variations of learning in, 12–21; type of learning that occurs in, 93–94. *See also* Adult learning communities; Practitioner inquiry communities
Community action groups, 18–21
Community development groups, 14–18
Community Futures 2010: case study describing, 27–28; connecting learning to social change, 37; description of origins of, 28–29; Six C model of learning in community and, 31–37; steering committee of, 32
Constructivist learning theory, 45–46
Continuing, 36–37
Contracting, 33–34
Contributing, 34–35
Cosier, J., 31
Coterie, The, (woman's club), 10, 13, 19–20
Cousineau, P., 76
Cranton, P., 55
Creating local knowledge, 28
Creativity and Adult Education (Edelson), 76
Cremin, L., 9
Cyberspace learning communities, 88–90

Daft, R. L., 55
Day, D., 19
de Geus, A., 51, 55, 56
Deshler, D., 8
Dewey, J., 15, 18
Drennon, C. E., 61, 62, 71, 95, 96
Duffy, T. M., 93
Duhl, H., 29

Easter, O., 19
"Ecology of education," 9
Edelson, P., 76
Effrate, M., 5
Elden, M., 30
Empowerment, 54–55
Essert, P., 16
Experimental College (University of Wisconsin), 15
External learning network, 52

Facilitators: dealing with power/politics inside of group, 63–64; dealing with power/politics outside of group, 64–65; negotiating group identity/knowledge creation, 67–68; negotiating power issues/politics, 65–66; negotiating social/organizational identity, 66–67; role of Yukon Island, 77–78. *See also* Practitioner inquiry communities
Farm Forum radio programs (Canada), 16
Fieldhouse, R., 5, 11
Fleek, B., 80
Ford Foundation, 16
Foucault, M., 64
Fout, S., 33, 35
Franklin, B., 12
Freire, P., 19, 20
Fryer, H., 38
Future search methodology, 333

Gabelnick, F., 15, 16
Garvey, M., 19
Gemeinschaft (community)-*gesellschaft* (society) continuum, 7, 8, 21
Giroux, H. A., 55
Glennie, S., 31
Goldberger, N. R., 87
Goleman, D., 56
Goodman, R., 31
Gore, J. M., 64, 68
Gratton, C. H., 7, 12
Gray, B., 41, 43–44
Great Books program, 16
Grossman, W., 29
Guy, T., 16
Gyant, L., 16

"Habitats of knowledge," 9
Handbook for the Soul (Andrews, Carson, and Shield), 75
Hart, J. K., 15

Hart, M., 20
Head Start, 32
Health Watch 2000, 28, 29
Heaney, T., 18, 19, 20, 93
Heidrich, K., 32
Heitmann, J., 32
Heron, J., 29, 95
Hiemstra, R., 16, 17
Highlander Folk School (Highlander Research and Education Center), 18–19
Holbrook, J., 12
Holly, P., 68
Horizontal learning network, 52
Horizontal learning organizations, 53
Horton, M., 18, 20, 86
Hugo, J. M., 5, 6, 10, 14, 19, 20, 22, 25, 95, 96
Hull House (Chicago), 16
Human capital theory, 17, 20
Hutchins, R., 16

Imel, S., 8, 9, 41, 42, 47, 49, 93, 94, 95, 97
Inquiry groups. *See* Practitioner inquiry communities

Jacques, R., 51
Janoff, S., 32, 33
Jarvis, P., 5, 7, 8, 10
Johnson, K., 29
Johnson, V., 78
Junto (Philadelphia discussion circle), 12

Keane, P., 5, 12, 18, 19
Kegler, M., 35
Kemmis, S., 61, 64
Kett, J., 12, 15, 16, 20
Knowledge: Common Good sharing of, 45; community participation in creating, 29–31; creating local, 28; cultural and historic component of, 30; habitats of, 9; as locally produced, 95; negotiating group identity and creation of, 67–68. *See also* Learning
Knowles, M., 16, 17
Kollock, P., 68
Kone, A., 32
Kornbluh, J. L., 18, 19
Korten, D. C., 53
Kotinsky, R., 1, 15, 18, 19
Kreuter, M., 37
Krieger, J., 32
Kubayashi, Y., 87

Lacy, W., 28, 95
Lakes, R., 20
Langone, C. A., 53
Lave, J., 93
Lawrence, R. L., 83, 84, 85, 89, 92, 94, 96
Learning: constructivist learning theory on, 45–46; implications of cohort groups for lifelong, 91; organizational, 53–57; relationship between community and content of, 94–95; role in success of Common Good team, 44–45; social learning theory on, 46; that occurs in community, 93–94. *See also* Adult learning communities; Knowledge
Learning from the CEO: How Chief Executives Shape Corporate Education (Meister), 54
Learning in community: community participation in, 29–31; connecting community social change to, 37; meaning of, 27; Six C model of, 31–37
Learning networks, 52–53
Learning organic, 78
Lengel, R. H., 55
Lezin, N., 37
Liberal learning network, 52–53
Linderman, E., 11–12, 15, 18, 19, 22
Little, J., 68
Living company concept, 55
Living Room Learning (University of British Columbia), 16
Longworth, N., 29, 38, 93
Lund, C. L., 73, 81, 94, 95
Lyceum movement (1830–1860), 12
Lytle, S. L., 61, 68, 69

MacGregor, J., 15
Maher, F. A., 66
Malcolm, J., 93
Malek, S., 35
Marshall, D., 74
Marsick, V. J., 13, 17, 47, 48, 95
Mattessich, P. W., 41, 43, 44
Matthews, R., 15, 16
Maurin, P., 19
McIntosh, D-B., 77, 80
McLeroy, K., 35
Mealman, C. A., 85
The Meaning of Adult Education (Linderman), 11
Meiklejohn, A., 15, 16
Meister, J. C., 51, 53

Merriam, S. B., 45, 46
Middletown (Lynds), 15
Mills, D. P., 53
Monsey, B. A., 41, 43, 44
Moran, L., 51
Moshi, L., 54
Mott Foundation, 16
Musselwhite, E., 51

Noffke, S., 64

O'Brien, J., 68
Ohio Department of Health, 28
Ohio Department of Human Services, 28
Oliver, L., 16
Organic learning, 78
Organizational learning: critical awareness versus surplus control of, 55–56;
empowerment of, 54–55; organizational lacunae versus, 56–57; power
interests and agenda of, 53
Organizational learning communities:
championing new values, 58; contradictions in learning quest in, 55–57;
corporate universities as instruments
of control, 53–54; creating a vision in,
57; forms and names of, 51–52; horizontal, 53; language of power in, 54;
learning networks as, 52–53; learning
as technology of power in, 54–55;
power interests and learning agenda
of, 53; self-deception of, 57; staying on
focus, 58
Orsburn, J. D., 51
Overstreet, B., 15
Overstreet, H., 15
Owenby, P. H., 51, 60, 95

Palloff, R. M., 5, 88
Palmer, P., 75
Poell, R. F., 51, 52, 53
Popkewitz, T. S., 64
Posch, P., 61
Power: inside practitioner inquiry communities, 63–64; negotiating politics and
issues of inquiry group, 65–66; organizational learning community and language of, 54; organizational learning as
technology of, 54–55; outside of practitioner inquiry communities, 64–65
Powershift issues, 57
Practitioner inquiry communities: images
of and experience with, 61–63; negotiating power issues/politics of, 65–66;

negotiating public identity of, 68–69;
negotiating social/organization identity
of, 66–67; power and politics inside of,
63–64; power and politics outside of,
64–65. *See also* Facilitators
Pratt, K., 5, 88
Progressive Era reform, 10–11, 14–15,
17, 18, 22
Putnam, R., 6, 8, 10, 22

Quest, A. W., 79, 81

Rawls, J., 56
Reason, P., 29, 30
Rees, E. F., 54
Regime of truth discourse, 64
Remote retreat learning communities:
catalysts for change in, 79–80; collab-
oration in, 79; community building of,
77; facilitator and learner roles in,
77–78; lessons of, 80–81; locus of
control in, 76–77; organic learning in,
78; Yukon Island, 73–76
Reumann, R., 61
Rocco, T., 66
Rockefeller Foundation, 16
Rockhill, K., 5, 11
Rogers, M., 13
Rose, A. D., 6, 20

St. Clair, R., 5, 6, 51, 95
Saltiel, I., 79, 95
Schied, F. M., 17, 18, 20
Schorr, L. S., 42, 44
Schultz, T. W., 20
Scott, A. F., 7
Second wave world, 55
Self-ethnic reliance philosophy, 19
Selle, P., 32
Senge, P., 45
Senturia, K., 32
Sgroi, A., 79, 95
She-She-She Camps, 19
Six C model of learning: campaigning
and, 34; committing and, 31–33; com-
municating and, 35–36; continuing
and, 36–37; contracting and, 33–34;
contributing, 34–35
Sklar, K. K., 11
Smith, B., 15, 16
Smith, H. W., 19
Snyder, W., 27, 46
Social change, 37
Social learning theory, 46

Social movements, 18–21
Somekh, B., 61
Stamps, D., 46
Steckler, A., 35
Stein, D. S., 27, 40, 93, 94, 95, 96, 97
Stein, M. R., 10, 19
Stubblefield, H., 5, 12, 15, 16, 18, 19
Sullivan, M., 32
Surplus order, 56
Susman, W., 11
Sussmuth, R., 93

Tarule, J. M., 87
Taylor, R., 5, 11
Taylorism (early 1900s), 17
Teachers. See Adult educators
Tetreault, M.K.T., 66
Third wave world, 55, 57
Tisdell, E. J., 53, 66, 67
Toffler, A., 55, 56, 57
Tönnies, F., 7, 8
Turkle, S., 90

University of Wisconsin Experimental College, 15
USENET Internet discussion groups, 53

Van der Krogt, F. J., 51, 52, 53
van der Veen, R., 13, 17
Vertical learning networks, 52
Volpe, M., 95

Warmerdam, J.H.M., 59
Warren, C., 85
Watkins, K., 47, 48
Weinstock, J. A., 22
Weisbord, M., 32, 33
Wenger, E., 27, 46, 93
West, G. W., 66
Wheatley, M., 93
Whipple, W. R., 85
WIA (Workforce Investment Act) [1998], 42
Wildemeerch, D., 51, 52
Wilson, A. L., 6, 21, 53, 54, 65, 66
Wlodkowski, R., 75, 80
Wood, D. J., 41, 43–44

Young, L., 37
Yukon Island Center for Research and Education, 73
Yukon Island learning community: background environment of, 73–74; basic comforts of, 74–75; climate of trust in, 75–76; lessons from, 80–81; natural setting of, 74

Zeichner, K. M., 64, 68
Zenger, J. H., 51
Zengler, C. J., 41, 42, 47, 49, 94, 95, 96
Zuboff, S., 18
Zukas, M., 93

Back Issue/Subscription Order Form

Copy or detach and send to:

Jossey-Bass, A Wiley Company, 989 Market Street, San Francisco CA 94103-1741

Call or fax toll-free: Phone 888-378-2537 6AM-5PM PST; Fax 888-481-2665

Back issues: Please send me the following issues at $27 each

(Important: please include series initials and issue number, such as ACE90)

1. ACE _____

_____

_____

$ _____Total for single issues

$ _____ SHIPPING CHARGES: SURFACE

	Domestic	Canadian
First Item	$5.00	$6.50
Each Add'l Item	$3.00	$3.00

For next-day and second-day delivery rates, call the number listed above.

Subscriptions: Please ❑ start ❑ renew my subscription to *New Directions for Adult and Continuing Education* for the year 2____ at the following rate:

U.S.	❑ Individual $65	❑ Institutional $135
Canada	❑ Individual $65	❑ Institutional $175
All Others	❑ Individual $89	❑ Institutional $209

$ _____Total single issues and subscriptions (Add appropriate sales tax for your state for single issue orders. No sales tax for U.S. subscriptions. Canadian residents, add GST for subscriptions and single issues.)

Federal Tax ID 135593032   GST 89102 8052

❑ Payment enclosed (U.S. check or money order only)

❑ VISA, MC, AmEx, Discover Card # _____ Exp. date_____

Signature _____ Day phone _____

❑ Bill me (U.S. institutional orders only. Purchase order required)

Purchase order #_____

Name _____

Address _____

_____

Phone_____ E-mail _____

For more information about Jossey-Bass, visit our Web site at: www.josseybass.com

PROMOTION CODE = ND3

ACE94   **Collaborative Inquiry as a Strategy for Adult Learning**
Lyle Yorks, Elizabeth Kasl
Examines the practice of collaborative inquiry (CI), a systematic process that
educators can use to help adults make meaning from their experience,
through richly detailed case descriptions. Highlights particular
characteristics of the authors' projects so that this volume, taken as a whole,
represents the diversity of issues important to adult educators. Provides
guidance to adult educators while at the same time adding to the emerging
discourse about this process.
0-7879-6322-4

ACE93   **Contemporary Viewpoints on Teaching Adults Effectively**
Jovita Ross-Gordon
The aim of this sourcebook was to bring together several authors who have
contributed through their recent publications to the recent literature on
effective teaching of adults. Rather than promoting a single view of what
constitutes good teaching of adults, the chapters challenge each of us to
reflect on our beliefs regarding teaching and learning along with our
understandings of adults learners, the teaching-learning environment, and
the broader social context within which adult continuing education takes
place.
0-7879-6229-5

ACE92 **Sociocultural Perspectives on Learning through Work**
Tara Fenwick
Offers an introduction to current themes among academic researchers who
are interested in sociocultural understandings of work-based learning and
working knowledge—how people learn in and through everyday activities
that they think of as work. Explores how learning is embedded in the social
relationships, cultural dynamics, and politics of work, and recommends
different ways for educators to be part of the process.
ISBN 0-7879-5775-5

ACE91   **Understanding and Negotiating the Political Landscape of Adult Education**
Catherine A. Hansman, Peggy A. Sissel
Provides key insights into the politics and policy issues in adult education
today. Offering effective strategies for reflection and action, chapters explore
issues in examination and negotiation of the political aspects of higher
education, adult educators in K-12-focused colleges of education, literacy
education, social welfare reform, professional organizations, and identity of
the field.
ISBN 0-7879-5775-5

ACE90   **Promoting Journal Writing in Adult Education**
Leona M. English, Marie A. Gillen
Exploring the potential for personal growth and learning through journal
writing for student and mentor alike, this volume aims to establish journal
writing as an integral part of the teaching and learning process. Offers

examples of how journal writing can be, and has been, integrated into educational areas as diverse as health education, higher education, education for women, and English as a Second Language.
ISBN 0-7879-5774-7

ACE89   The New Update on Adult Learning Theory
Sharan B. Merriam
A companion work to 1993's popular An Update on Adult Learning Theory, this issue examines the developments, research, and continuing scholarship in self-directed learning. Exploring context-based learning, informal and incidental learning, somatic learning, and narrative learning; the authors analyze recent additions to well-established theories and discuss the potential impact of today's cutting-edge approaches.
ISBN 0-7879-5773-9

ACE88   Strategic Use of Learning Technologies
Elizabeth J. Burge
The contributors draw on case examples to explore the advantages and disadvantages of three existing learning technologies—print, radio, and the Internet—and examine how a large urban university has carefully combined old and new technologies to provide a range of learner services tailored to its enormous and varied student body.
ISBN 0-7879-5426-8

ACE87   Team Teaching and Learning in Adult Education
Mary-Jane Eisen, Elizabeth J. Tisdell
The contributors show how team teaching can increase both organizational and individual learning in settings outside of a traditional classroom, for example, a recently deregulated public utility, a national literacy organization, and community-based settings such as Chicago's south side. They discuss how team teaching can be used in colleges and universities, describing strategies for administrators and teachers who want to integrate it into their curricula and classrooms.
ISBN 0-7879-5425-X

ACE86   Charting a Course for Continuing Professional Education: Reframing Professional Practice
Vivian W. Mott, Barbara J. Daley
This volume offers a resource to help practitioners examine and improve professional practice, and set new directions for the field of CPE across multiple professions. The contributors provide a brief review of the development of the field of CPE, analyze significant issues and trends that are shaping and changing the field, and propose a vision of the future of CPE.
ISBN 0-7879-5424-1

ACE85   Addressing the Spiritual Dimensions of Adult Learning: What Educators Can Do
Leona M. English, Marie A. Gillen
The contributors discuss how mentoring, self-directed learning, and dialogue can be used to promote spiritual development, and advocate the learning covenant as a way of formalizing the sanctity of the bond between learners and educators. Drawing on examples from continuing professional

education, community development, and health education, they show how a spiritual dimension has been integrated into adult education programs.
ISBN 0-7879-5364-4

ACE84 **An Update on Adult Development Theory: New Ways of Thinking About the Life Course**
M. Carolyn Clark, Rosemary J. Caffarella
This volume presents discussions of well-established theories and new perspectives on learning in adulthood. Knowles' andragogy, self-directed learning, Mezirow's perspective transformation, and several other models are assessed for their contribution to our understanding of adult learning. In addition, recent theoretical orientations, including consciousness and learning, situated cognition, critical theory, and feminist pedagogy, are discussed in terms of how each expands the knowledge base of adult learning.
ISBN 0-7879-1171-2

ACE83 **The Welfare-to-Work Challenge for Adult Literacy Educators**
Larry G. Martin, James C. Fisher
Welfare reform and workforce development legislation has had a dramatic impact on the funding, implementation, and evaluation of adult basic education and literacy programs. This issue provides a framework for literacy practitioners to better align their field with the demands of the Work First environment and to meet the pragmatic expectations of an extended list of stakeholders.
ISBN 0-7879-1170-4

ACE82 **Providing Culturally Relevant Adult Education: A Challenge for the Twenty-First Century**
Talmadge C. Guy
This issue offers more inclusive theories that focus on how learners construct meaning in a social and cultural context. Chapters identify ways that adult educators can work more effectively with racially, ethnically, and linguistically marginalized learners, and explore how adult education can be an effective tool for empowering learners to take control of their circumstances.
ISBN 0-7879-1167-4

ACE81 **Enhancing Creativity in Adult and Continuing Education: Innovative Approaches, Methods, and Ideas**
Paul Jay Edelson, Patricia L. Malone
The authors discuss innovations in a variety of continuing education settings, including the Harvard Institute for the Management of Lifelong Education; a drug and alcohol prevention program; and a college degree program developed through the collaboration of the Bell Atlantic Corporation and a consortium of community colleges.
ISBN 0-7879-1169-0

ACE79 **The Power and Potential of Collaborative Learning Partnerships**
Iris M. Saltiel, Angela Sgroi, Ralph G. Brockett
This volume draws on examples of collaborative partnerships to explore the many ways collaboration can generate learning and knowledge. The

contributors identify the factors that make for strong collaborative relationships, and they reveal how these partnerships actually help learners generate knowledge and insights well beyond what each brings to the learning situation.
ISBN 0-7879-9815-X

ACE78   Adult Learning and the Internet
Brad Cahoon
This volume explores the effects of the Internet on adult learning—both as that learning is facilitated through formal instruction and as it occurs spontaneously in the experiences of individuals and groups—and provides guidance to adult and continuing educators searching for ways to use the Internet effectively in their practice.
ISBN 0-7879-1166-6

ACE77   Using Learning to Meet the Challenges of Older Adulthood
James C. Fisher, Mary Alice Wolf
Combining theory and research in educational gerontology with the practice of older adult learning and education, this volume explores issues related to older adult education in academic and community settings. It is designed for educators and others concerned with the phenomenon of aging in America and with the continuing development of the field of educational gerontology.
ISBN 0-7879-1164-X

ACE75   Assessing Adult Learning in Diverse Settings: Current Issues and Approaches
Amy D. Rose, Meredyth A. Leahy
Examines assessment approaches analytically from different programmatic levels and looks at the implications of these differing approaches. Chapters discuss the implications of cultural differences as well as ideas about knowledge and knowing and the implications these ideas can have for both the participant and the program.
ISBN 0-7879-9840-0

ACE73   Creating Practical Knowledge Through Action Research: Posing Problems, Solving Problems, and Improving Daily Practice
B. Allan Quigley, Gary W. Kuhne
Outlines the process of action research step-by-step, provides a convenient project planner, and presents examples to show how action research yielded improvements in six different settings, including a hospital, a university, and a literacy education program.
ISBN 0-7879-9841-9

ACE70   A Community-Based Approach to Literacy Programs: Taking Learners' Lives into Account
Peggy A. Sissel
Encouraging a community-based approach that takes account of the reality of learner's lives; this volume offers suggestions for incorporating knowledge about a learner's particular context, culture, and community into adult literacy programming.
ISBN 0-7879-9867-2

ACE69   What Really Matters in Adult Education Program Planning: Lessons in
        Negotiating Power and Interests
        Ronald M. Cervero, Arthur L. Wilson
        Identifies issues faced by program planners in practice settings and the
        actual negotiation strategies they use. Argues that planning is generally
        conducted within a set of personal, organizational, and social relationships
        among people who may have similar, different, or conflicting interests and
        the program planner's responsibility centers on how to negotiate these
        interests to construct an effective program.
        ISBN 0-7879-9866-4

ACE66   Mentoring: New Strategies and Challenges
        Michael W. Galbraith, Norman H. Cohen
        Assists educators in clarifying and describing various elements of the
        mentoring process. Also intended to enhance the reader's understanding of
        the utility, practice application, and research potential of mentoring in adult
        and continuing education.
        ISBN 0-7879-9912-1

ACE62   Experiential Learning: A New Approach
        Lewis Jackson, Rosemary S. Caffarella
        This volume presents discussions of a comprehensive model of experiential
        learning for instructors of adults in formal educational programs. Chapters
        argue that linking the conceptual foundations of adult and experimental
        learning to actual instructional applications is key to effective practice.
        ISBN 0-7879-9956-3

ACE59   Applying Cognitive Learning Theory to Adult Learning
        Daniele D. Flannery
        While much is written about adult learning, basic tenets of cognitive theory
        are often taken for granted. This volume presents an understanding of basic
        cognitive theory and applies it to the teaching-learning exchange.
        ISBN 1-55542-716-2

ACE57   An Update on Adult Learning Theory
        Sharan B. Merriam
        This volume presents discussions of well-established theories and new
        perspectives on learning in adulthood. Knowles' andragogy, self-directed
        learning, Mezirow's perspective transformation, and several other models are
        assessed for their contribution to our understanding of adult learning.
        ISBN 1-55542-684-0